Targeting Violence
In Our Schools:
Thinking Towards Solutions

Targeting Violence
In Our Schools:
Thinking Towards Solutions

Brenda Guenther LeTendre

and

Richard P. Lipka

Christopher-Gordon Publishers, Inc.
Norwood, Massachusetts

Copyright Acknowledgments

Every effort has been made to contact copyright holders for permission to reproduce borrowed material where necessary. We apologize for any oversights and would be happy to rectify them in future printings.

LeTendre, B. (Winter 2000). "Six Steps to a Solution." *Journal of Staff Development* 21,(1). Reprinted with permission of the National Staff Development Council, 2002. All rights reserved.

Christopher-Gordon Publishers, Inc.
1502 Providence Highway, Suite #12
Norwood, Massachusetts 02062
800-934-8322
781-762-5577

Printed in the United State of America
10 9 8 7 6 5 4 3 2 1   07 06 05 04 03

ISBN: 1-929024-62-2
Library of Congress Catalogue Number: 20033104431

Acknowledgments

A book such as this rests on the efforts, suggestions, and ideas of many others besides the authors. First, we thank the reviewers who provided valuable suggestions on how to make this book more reader-friendly and useful: Ida Cabral, James C. Christman, Catherine de Boer, John Fagan, Sandra Fehr, David Kroeze, Ida Malian, and Kathleen Meadows. All highlighted both the strengths and weaknesses of earlier drafts and gave us guidance in how to better organize the chapters and clarify the concepts we present. Also, we say "thank you" to Dana LeTendre, Brenda's husband, who provided useful editing on the last drafts of this book.

Next, we give a special thanks to Mark Galley, a consultant with ThinkReliability.com. His presentation at the 2002 United School Administrators of Kansas annual conference sparked the move to include an explicit systems approach within the *Targeted Problem-Solving* process showcased in this book. He also spurred us to include cause mapping as a tool for visually capturing the deliberations of groups as they grapple with issues of violence within their classrooms and schools. Finally, throughout the early drafts of this book, Mark offered invaluable suggestions and direction on how to improve our explanations of the problem-solving process. His outsider's view, as a reliability engineer more familiar with industry than the day-to-day workings of schools along with his concerns as a parent, caused us to more carefully hone our concepts to the needs of all members of the school community, educators, parents, and students.

Finally, we express thanks to Sue Canavan at Christopher-Gordon Publishers for her continued encouragement and support throughout this writing project. She not only provided constructive suggestions, but also buoyed us up as we worked to create this book.

Short Table of Contents

Expanded Table of Contents

List of Figures

Part I

Part II

Part III

Part IV

Part I

Introduction

School Violence: Where we stand today

2 Dead, 6 Wounded in Kentucky High School Shooting[1]

"I never dreamed it would happen here"

> December 1, 1997
> Heath High School, West Paducah, Kentucky
> 3 killed, 5 wounded

False Fire Alarm Led Pupils, Staff into Gunfire[2]

Triage doctor horrified

> March 24, 1998
> Westside Middle School, Jonesboro, Arkansas
> 5 dead, 10 wounded

School Library Full of Shooting Victims[3]

> April 20, 1999
> Columbine High School, Littleton, Colorado
> 15 dead, 18 wounded

Boy, 13, Wounds 4 in School Shooting[4]

December 6, 1999
Fort Gibson Middle School, Fort Gibson, Oklahoma
0 killed, 4 wounded

2 killed, 13 hurt in school shooting[5]

March 6, 2001
Santana High School, Santee, California
2 killed, 13 wounded

Expelled Student Kills 17, Self at School in Germany[6]

April 26, 2002
Johann Gutenberg Gymnasium
Erfurt, Germany
18 killed

In the past years such headlines have occurred all too frequently. Indeed, since 1996, over 30 students in the United States have died at the hands of their classmates within the hallways and classrooms of their schools.[7] Such horrific events have ravaged the sense of safety that both students and adults once felt about schools. A nationwide poll conducted by CNN/USA Today/ Gallup the day after the Columbine shootings showed that 55% of the parents in the sample feared for their child's safety while at school.[8] This same poll revealed that 68% of the respondents felt that similar school shootings could likely happen in their communities.[9] Although parents' fears have subsided somewhat as schools hurriedly implemented increased security measures, parents still rank violence as one of their top concerns.[10]

While most students say they feel safe at school, various surveys indicate that as many as 25% say they avoid certain places at school because they fear someone might hurt or bother them.[11] Furthermore, additional surveys reveal that 6 to 8% skip school because they feel unsafe.[12]

School violence, unfortunately, is not a new phenomenon. With only periodic slight dips and peaks, the level of violent crime reported by schools from 1976 to 1998 has remained steady over the past quarter-century. Over the years, about 5% of high school seniors said they had been injured with a weapon, while about 12% reported they had been injured by means other than a weapon. About 15% had been threatened with a weapon and about 20% had been threatened without a weapon. Consistently, a high percentage of high school seniors indicated that they had been victims of property crimes, with about 40% saying that they had something stolen from them while at school.[13]

Before the massacre at Columbine High School, the American public viewed school violence as existing only within urban schools situated in high-poverty, high-crime areas. Thus, such violence rarely made national headlines. When it did, the news stories talked about gang warfare spilling onto the school grounds or news reporters told of a demented adult entering a school, killing, and maiming.

Columbine High School, however, dramatically altered the nation's image of school violence. Rather than gangs or a demented adult perpetrating the violence, two students from white, upper-middle–class suburban homes went on a rampage that ended with 15 dead, 18 wounded, and untold numbers of students and adults psychologically damaged. No longer did bloody violence appear to occur only within the inner cities. Now, even schools like Columbine, sitting in affluent suburbs or in quiet small towns, have to contend with the possibility that "it could happen here."

Window-Dressing and Cookie-Cutter Solutions

After each terrible event (Columbine, Jonesboro, Fort Gibson, Santana), the country cried a collective "Why?" Publicly and privately, adults wondered about the home life of the violent perpetrators, about their mental health, about their drug use. Some even wondered if the schools themselves might have somehow contributed to these terrible events.

Parents clamored for immediate responses and school officials complied. Rather than address the "whys," or underlying causes of the violence, most officials, both within the government and schools, frequently opted for quick fixes, often implementing window-dressing and cookie-cutter solutions that focused only on symptoms. Many schools took a defensive rather than a pro-active stance.

So today we find the following:

- 49 states and the U.S. Congress, have passed legislation requiring zero tolerance of weapons on school grounds with mandatory long-term suspension or expulsion of violators.[14]

- 80% of middle school and high school students in the United States attend schools that have enacted get-tough, zero-tolerance discipline codes.[15]

- 15% of American schools have surveillance cameras within their buildings.[16]

- 23% of U.S. high schools have armed police officers or security guards assigned to their campuses.[17]

- 96% of U.S. schools require visitors to sign in as they enter the building.[18]

- 9% of U.S. secondary schools use metal detectors to randomly check students.[19]

- 2% of U.S. secondary students must pass through metal detectors each day.[20]

In some cases, these strategies provided a much needed step forward in boosting physical safety in schools. In other cases, however, such security measures represented only "window-dressing solutions" that simply made the public and school community members *feel* "we are doing something." None of these measures addressed the underlying causes of violence within most schools.

For example, one of the authors visited a midwestern school that overlooks rolling pasture land, miles from the nearest town or farm house. The school's nearest neighbors consist of grazing dairy cows. Shortly after the Columbine incident, this school, in an effort to improve its "lax" security, constructed an eight-foot, chain-link fence worthy of a high-security military installation around its campus. Furthermore, the school's principal had workers mount surveillance cameras throughout the hallways. Meanwhile, the principal and faculty continued to tolerate pervasive bullying and harassment among the upper-grade students.

Such misplaced efforts to improve security while ignoring the causes of violence also illustrate the "cookie-cutter, one-size-fits-all" mentality that characterized the responses that many schools made after Columbine. Elected officials and school administrators tended to grab at the first "solutions" that came to mind, whether or not these measures actually fit with a school's particular context. Thus, we ended up with security fences and surveillance cameras in schools that really needed entirely different strategies to successfully address the unique causes of violence within their school communities. Indeed, U.S. Surgeon General David Satcher stressed that "Certain hastily adopted and implemented strategies may be ineffective—and even deleterious—for all children and youth."[21]

Good News, Bad News

When it comes to school violence, the reality is a classic case of good news/bad news. The good news is horrendous events such as mass shootings rarely occur. Despite the public's perception that school violence has taken a sharp increase, the reality is that violent crime in schools declined slightly in the 1990s.[22] Furthermore, the chances of a shooting occurring at school are extremely low.[23]

But the bad news is that youngsters in many schools face a daily "climate of fear" filled with bullying, verbal harassment, intimidation, physical aggression, public humiliation, and vicious rumors.[24] In 2001, data collected as part of the Safe and Drug-Free Schools and Communities Act indicated that 18% of the middle school students and 10% of the high school students had suffered a physical attack while at school.[25] On this same survey, almost 25% said they avoided specific places around their schools out of fear that someone might hurt or bother them.[26] Furthermore, the *Indicators of School Crime and Safety, 2002* reported that 8% said they had been bullied at school during the prior six months.[27] Finally, 36% indicated they saw hate-related graffiti on their school grounds, while 12% reported being the targets of hate-related words.[28]

The Iceberg of Violence in our Schools

School violence comes in two varieties:

1. Criminal acts of violence, such as murder, assault, shooting, or sexual assault; and

2. Everyday acts of violence that not only create a "climate of fear" that impedes learning, but can also serve as antecedents to more violent criminal acts.[29]

Although such events capture the national and international headlines, school shootings like the massacres at Columbine High School and Jonesboro Middle School rarely happen and represent only the tip of an "iceberg" of daily violent acts that occur in schools.

Figure I.1   The Iceberg of School Violence

Criminal Acts of Violence

Daily Acts of Violence
Bullying
Verbal harrassment
Intimidation
Physical threats
Public humiliation
Vicious rumor mongering

These daily acts of violence, however, have both immediate and lingering negative effects on students. We know from brain research that threat (real or perceived) hinders a student's ability to learn.[30] A student who knows that when the bell rings he must pass through a gauntlet of bullies in the hallway, simply cannot concentrate on learning algebra. A female student who controls her fluid intake all day because she fears going into the girls' bathroom, finds herself, by the end of the day, more focused on her own bodily needs than on a biology teacher's lecture on human anatomy.

These adverse effects extend even into adulthood. A group of 23 year-olds who reported being victims of bullying at age 16 showed higher levels of depression and negative self-esteem when compared to a similar group of 23 year-olds who had not endured such violence.[31]

These negative consequences of everyday violence do not affect only the victims. Those who perpetrate the violence and those who stand by and watch violence occur also suffer, but in different ways. Recent research shows that perpetrators of school violence lack leadership qualities and often resort to physical power and physical action as problem-solving strategies. As they grow into adulthood, they continue these same aggressive behaviors and demonstrate a strong need for dominance and power.[32]

Those who observe violence also suffer. Bystanders to school violence indicate they feel increased anxiety. They must spend time looking over their shoulders lest they become the next victims. This toxic combination of anxiety and vigilance makes academic achievement difficult and school absenteeism likely.[33]

It's these more frequent and pervasive daily acts of violence—physical aggression, verbal abuse, humiliation, rumor mongering, bullying, and taunting—that the quick-fix solutions to beef up security do not, indeed cannot, remedy. To reduce or eliminate this daily violence, educators must look beyond the quick fixes and, instead, dig deep to discover the underlying causes of such behavior. Only then can they craft effective solutions to reduce violence within their schools.

Intelligent Responses to Violence

This leads us to our reasons for writing this book. As authors, we come from different backgrounds and perspectives and yet we share a common commitment:

> We believe that all children and teens have the right to experience a learning environment free of physical and psychological threat.

Our chief aim in writing this book is to help you, as an educator, concerned parent, or community member, find ways to reduce the probability of violence occurring in your school. We want to help you reduce the likelihood that a criminal act of violence will happen in your school *and* we want to help you reduce the level of everyday violence that currently takes place within your school. In other words, we want to help you create a physically and emotionally safe environment where all students can learn.

Furthermore, we hope to guide you in finding intelligent responses to school violence, responses that can effectively tackle the violence issues within *your* own school. Finally, we want to help you use your scarce resources wisely by helping you to identify the causes of violence and find effective strategies for addressing those causes.

What This Book Will Do

In this book, we won't provide a list of violence-prevention interventions, strategies, or programs guaranteed to work in all settings. Furthermore, we won't recommend the definitive solution to school violence. If you are looking for the *one* right way of preventing violence in all schools, then, in our judgment, you're looking for the wrong thing.

However, in this book, we will do the following:

- We will instruct you in a process for thinking through violence issues at *your* school.

- We will show you how to use this process, which we call *Targeted Problem-Solving*, illustrating each step of the way with two case studies, one from a middle school and another from a high school.

- We will teach you how to use root-cause analysis to identify the causes of violence within *your* school.

- We will demonstrate the power of systems thinking in combating violence within *your* school.

- Finally, we will guide you in developing an action plan tailored for *your* school that:

    (1) decreases the level of everyday violence; and

    (2) reduces the possibility of criminal acts of violence occurring.

In Part II, we introduce *Targeted Problem-Solving* and demonstrate how a team of sixth-grade teachers used the process to confront fighting and teasing among their students. In Part III, we give another example of *Targeted Problem-Solving* at work. This time, we show how a high school tackled the bullying among female students.

Finally, Part IV offers further help. The Tool Kit provides forms and guides that you can photocopy or download from our website to help you in your deliberations. Here we also describe resources we have available on our website to assist you as you tackle violence in your school. Finally, Appendix A rounds out the book with an article from the *Journal of Staff Development*, showing you how to evaluate the effectiveness of your solutions.

Prevention Works Best

Before we go much further, we wish to state a basic premise that forms the foundation of this book: Prevention works best. Yes, at times you will find yourself in a reactive mode using *Targeted Problem-Solving* to discover what went wrong and how you can reduce violence within your school. Indeed, in Parts II and III, we show a team of teachers and an entire school community start-ing in just such a reactive mode. However, they soon recognized they must look beyond the current incidents and take a more proactive, preventative stance.

A series of violent incidents may serve as a wake-up call and get us to focus on doing something about a festering problem, but the damage is done. Better to focus on preventing violence than simply reacting to it when it happens.

Focusing on prevention requires that we turn our attention to the seeds of violence. First, we know that certain *everyday behaviors* tend to breed more violence and sometimes escalate to more violent criminal acts. For example, those who commit crimes as young adults often bullied others when they were children.[34] Furthermore, the victims of bullies can sometimes lash out in retaliation with awful results. After examining 37 of the most recent school shootings, the U.S. Secret Service reported that a majority of the shooters had suffered at the hands of bullies.[35]

We also know that certain *environmental factors* contribute to violence. Researchers have found that the following can all play a part in increasing violence within schools.

1. A physical layout that makes it difficult for adults to frequently and easily monitor students,

2. Hallways that create dangerous cross-traffic move-ment,

3. Inadequate lighting,

4. Large school size,

5. Large classes, and

6. Inadequate or nonexistent communication systems among the classrooms and adults in the building.[36]

Furthermore, studies suggest that many schools have certain "unowned areas" where no one, student or adult, takes responsi-bility for monitoring the space.[37] Often students see these areas as unsafe and, indeed, violence does often occur in these areas beyond the watchful eyes of faculty and staff.

Finally, certain aspects of the *organization* itself may also increase the probability of violence occurring within a school. All of the following may in some way contribute to the level of violence.

1. Policies, dictating such things as discipline codes, grading practices, and course content,

2. Procedures that focus more on control than personal responsibility,

3. Organizational structures such as the bell schedule, how we place students into classes, and where we locate certain classrooms,

4. Choices we make about what we monitor or ignore,

5. Expectations of students and adults for others and themselves,

6. Communication patterns: who communicates with whom, about what,

7. Social norms, such as a "don't-tell-the-adults" attitude among young people, and

8. Social networks, such as clearly defined social cliques that often clash with one another.[38]

Schools that fail to pay attention to these behavioral, physical, and organizational factors may find themselves sitting on a volcano of violence, ready to explode. For this reason, we suggest that schools take stock and focus on taking sensible precautions. Our website supporting this book at http://www.pittstate.edu/edsc/ssls/letendre.html includes several resources that can help you conduct a safety and climate audit of your school.

A System of Causes

Over the past three years, in the aftermath of several school shootings, people have tried to understand the unthinkable. Why did these students, most coming from economically privileged homes, walk into their schools and methodically massacre their classmates and teachers? People have sought to place blame on that one defining cause that set off the horrendous chain of events. But such attempts to place blame simply obscure the true complexity of these situations. Rarely can we talk about a linear chain of events with one cause setting off the chain reaction. Rather, we need to broaden our perspective and look not for *the* cause, but instead identify *a system of causes.*

In the previous section, we identified a host of factors that can contribute to violence within a school. It is, however, unlikely that any *one* of these seeds will grow into a criminal act. But these seeds can combine to create a weed patch that *does* increase the probability of criminal violence occurring.

An example that has nothing to do with schools can illustrate this cluster of causes at work. A car accident occurred one rainy night. The driver lost control as she rounded a curve and flipped her car, badly injuring herself and demolishing the car. The police, upon investigation, found that *all* of the following contributed to the accident.

- Bald tires,
- Poor visibility due to darkness,
- Rain slick roads,
- A sharp bend in the road, and
- Excessive speed as the car entered the curve.

Taken singly, none of these factors, on its own, significantly increased the probability of an accident. Even the driver's excessive speed by itself did not cause the accident. Yes, the speed increased the chances of having an accident, but, even if she had been driving at a slower rate of speed, she might not have safely negotiated the curve. The rain-slick highway, bald tires, and poor visibility still could have conspired to cause the accident. Clustered together, these five factors amplified her chances of having an accident. Indeed, clustered together these factors *did* cause the accident.

Figure I.2   Cause Map of Car Accident

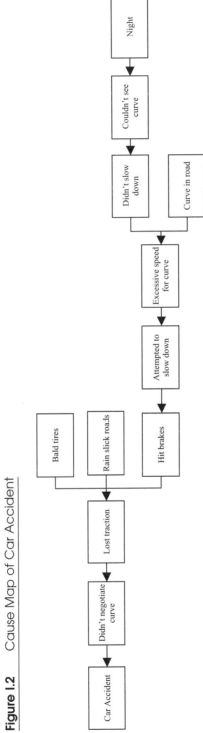

Whether we're examining a car accident, a school shooting incident, or a pervasive problem with bullying, the search for the phantom single cause leads us down a fruitless pathway. Complex problems, and even simple car accidents, have a *cluster* of causes. If we want to solve these complex problems, we must begin by looking at causes, not *the* cause.

"It Takes a Village:" A Systems Approach to Addressing School Violence

If we are to effectively reduce the incidence of violence within our schools, we must shift our thinking from looking for a phantom single cause to finding the cluster of causes that contribute to the problem. This is where systems thinking comes into play.

A familiar African proverb declares that "It takes a village to raise a child." Generally, people interpret this proverb as a call for all of us, regardless of our roles, to take responsibility for raising the children of our community. But we would like to suggest another interpretation. We see this proverb as embodying the essence of systems thinking. It acknowledges, indeed it highlights, the interconnectedness of *everyone* and *everything* in a "village." It's this interconnectedness that defines a system.

Simply put, a system is a combination of parts that interact and function as a whole. In general, the word system applies to a variety of common things in our world: highways; the weather; a manufacturing facility; telecommunications; a coffee maker; a business; and a school. With such a broad definition, we would have a hard time finding anything we would not classify as a system.

Not only do parts within a system interact and function as a whole, but each part also contributes equally to the system. A missing or faulty part will ripple through the system and cause the whole system to malfunction.

To easily demonstrate this systems approach, ask several people this question: "What is the most important part of a car?" You'll get answers ranging from the engine, to the transmission, to the key, to the steering wheel, to the battery. Actually, the question, "Which part of the car is the most important?" is a poor one. In reality, it takes *all* parts of a car, functioning *together* to be a car. A car is a system and no single part is more important than another.

Interestingly, if you ask your fellow educators which part of the school district is the most important, they will probably respond with the one in which they work. Elementary teachers will likely say, "Elementary school's the most important part. We lay the foundation," while high school science teachers will say "Science's the most important subject." Even bus drivers would say they are the most important because "if we don't get them to school, they can't learn!" Each group reasons, "if we don't do our job all of the other stuff won't matter."

But systems thinking forces us to see that all of us play an important role. All parts of the school or school district, not just some of us, must work together if we are to meet our goals and do right by the kids.

Zooming In and Zooming Out

Systems thinking requires that we not only see the interconnectedness of parts, but we also change our perspective as we examine different levels of a system. We begin by looking at a system as one large entity. Then we work our way down through various levels, as we break the large system down into smaller and smaller subsystems.

For example, to show a Powerpoint presentation during a workshop, a speaker may use a laptop computer, an LCD projector, and a screen. These three parts make up the "projection system." We can break these same three parts of the "projection system" into smaller systems. The computer, only one component in the "projection system," consists of the monitor, the keyboard, and the processing unit. At this level, we can think of the computer as a system on its own. It has parts that interact and function as a whole.

At the highest level, we defined our "projection system." One level down, we broke the projection system into a computer, a LCD projector, and a screen. Two levels down, we divided the laptop computer into its parts. As we progress from the highest level to the first and second levels down, we have moved from a macro perspective to an increasingly micro view.

MapQuest® and similar "driving directions" programs on the Internet provide an apt example of what we mean by these macro/micro viewpoints. After you type in your starting point and destination, the program will give you a map of your route. Then, with a click of your mouse, you can either zoom in for a more detailed (micro) street view or zoom out for a broader (macro) picture.

We can use this same zoom-in/zoom-out process with any system and any complex problem. Our ability to move back and forth through the levels, from macro to micro and back again, allows us to see problems at different levels, breaking down the complexities into more manageable parts and thus finding effective solutions to solve our problems.

For example, a fight occurs in a school's cafeteria. Two girls exchange heated words. The argument escalates to name-calling and a shoving match, with one of the girls knocking the other to the floor. All this happens as other students jump from their seats, surrounding the girls and inciting them to further violence.

From a zoom-in/micro viewpoint, you would examine this incident as something that occurred only between the two girls. What issue began the fight? What happened immediately before the girls got into the fight? Who started the shoving?

However, if you zoom out and take the macro perspective, you would examine the larger system of factors that contributed to the fight. Your questions at this level might include:

- What *student* attitudes in the school might have caused this fight?

- What cafeteria *procedures* might have contributed to this fight?

- What norms on the part of the school *adults* might have allowed this fight to occur?

This movement from the micro to macro view forces us to see the true complexity of the system of causes behind this one fight. It also encourages us to think more broadly about our solutions. Rather than simply stopping this one fight, we now can also focus on how to prevent future fights within the school. We move from dealing with the symptoms of the problem (the fight) to the system of causes of the problem.

If we wish to truly tackle the issues of school violence, we need to acquire this ability to both zoom in and zoom out as we view the problems. People who attempt to solve problems by looking at only *one* level often see only the details of a problem and miss the big picture. They can't see the forest for the trees! Conversely, other people fail to dig down through the levels within a problem and miss the complexity of causes. They don't see the trees! But systems thinking, coupled with the capacity to zoom in or zoom out, significantly improves the way we can communicate and analyze problems. Systems thinking allows us to see both the forest *and* the trees.

"Right Answer" Thinking vs. System Thinking

Just as some people get lost in the details and miss the big picture, others latch on that one phantom cause and its equally deceptive single solution. They get themselves tangled up in "right answer" thinking.

Let's look at two questions:

1. "What's the right answer to 2 + 7?" and

2. "How can we improve student safety in this school?"

A big difference exists between these two questions. Question (1) represents a "right answer" question. We all agree that 9 is the right answer to the first question. On the other hand, the second question indicates a systems problem—it has no single right answer. Also, it has no single cause. To find effective solutions, we need to consider many factors. Furthermore, we will need to craft a multipronged plan to really solve the problem of safety in a school.

Opening our minds to multiple causes and multiple solutions requires that we go against our cultural norms. So much of our training from early years and even into adulthood creates a bias toward right-answer thinking. Television's "Jeopardy" and similar game shows reward those who can get the "right" answer.

However, most of the real world does not function on one, right answer. We work and live in a world of primarily systems issues—with trade-offs, budgetary constraints, scheduling issues, deadlines, and resource limitations. Yet, many people, including those of us working in schools, approach systems issues with a right-answer frame of mind. Such a mismatch—working on a systems problem with a right-answer approach—can lead to difficulties. People miscommunicate, waste time and energy, and get defensive, all of which dampen our ability to solve pressing problems.

How do you know when a group is using "right-answer" thinking rather than systems thinking? You can simply listen to the language they use. With right-answer thinking, people say "right" or "wrong." With systems issues, people say words like, "good, better, and best."

Experiment with this systems approach yourself. Ask several people "What was the root cause of the *Titanic's* sinking?" Responses will differ, but each person will make the case that "My answer is right." People will say, "If _____ (their cause) never happened the *Titanic* would never have sunk."

What they are saying is true, but they are not "right." Right is a binary term—right or wrong. The *Titanic* incident is not a right-answer problem. Rather, it is a systems problem. The *Titanic* sank because of *a system of causes,* not a single cause. Removing any one of the causes from the system reduces the probability of occurrence but doesn't eliminate the problem altogether. Hitting the iceberg, sighting the iceberg too late, having a too-small rudder, and ignoring iceberg warnings all contributed to *Titanic's* sinking. By asking "What was *the* root cause?" we inappropriately pose a linear, right-answer question to a systems issue.

However, we don't want to leave you with the impression that you should never engage in right-answer thinking. Both methods, right-answer and systems thinking can serve us well when we apply them to the appropriate type of problem. For example, right-answer thinking works just fine for a problem like how many language arts sections do we need when we have 427 eighth graders enrolled.

But complex, multi-level problems require a systems approach. Linear, right-answer thinking only gets us so far. The common "Who? What? Where? When? and Why?" approach gets us off to a good start in determining cause and effect, but we must expand our thinking. We need to look for a system of causes rather than the one, single cause.

Root-Cause Analysis

In physics class we learned: "For every effect there is a cause." A more accurate definition of the cause and effect principle, however, is "For every effect there are *causes*." This subtle change produces a significant improvement in our ability to analyze problems.

Specifically, systems thinking, with its emphasis on taking both micro *and* macro views in analyzing a problem, encourages us to look for causes at all levels. Furthermore, it helps us identify those underlying causes that we so often miss because we get caught up in dealing with the surface causes, those factors we can readily identify because they're so obvious.

To identify the full range of causes (and eventually develop a set of solutions to alleviate these causes), we need to dig deep and look beyond the obvious, surface factors. This is where root-cause analysis comes into play.

Our front yards can provide a suitable example of root-cause analysis. When faced with a crop of weeds, we can't just remedy our weed problem by dealing with the surface cause that we see. If we just cut off the tops of the weeds, they will only grow back. We have to get to the roots if we really want to *solve* our weed problem. The surface leaves and the roots are part of the larger "weed" system. If we want to get rid of our weeds, we must remove the *roots*.

Figure I.3   The Weed System

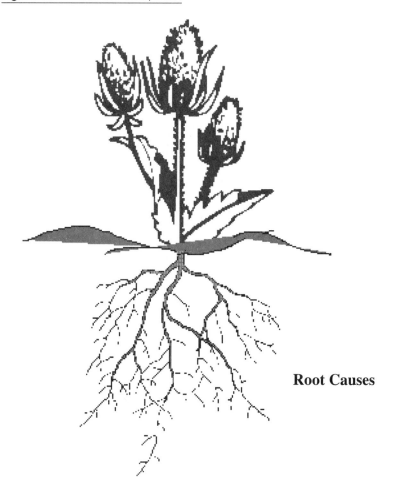

Root Causes

Our weed metaphor demonstrates the concept underlying root-cause analysis. In root-cause analysis we identify the *system of causes*. The focus of the analysis changes from who's "right" to what are the specific cause-and-effect relationships that created this issue.

In Part II, we will show how systems thinking and its related tool, root-cause analysis aided a team of sixth grade teachers as they grappled with fighting and bullying among their students.

You will see these educators dig through the levels of the system to identify the causes of the problem, taking both macro and micro views of the situation. We will also illustrate how these same educators used visual diagrams created in Microsoft® Excel to capture and share their thinking about this problem. Finally, we will show how they crafted a multipronged action plan to address the system of causes underlying the fights and bullying.

The Road Ahead

In Part I, we have laid the foundation for what will follow. We described the current context surrounding school violence, giving you a glimpse of the extent of the problem and how schools have tried to correct it. We also stated one of our central beliefs: Prevention works best. Finally, we introduced the concepts underlying systems thinking.

In Part II, we build on this foundation and show you step-by-step how to use *Targeted Problem-Solving* to think through the violence issues you face in your classroom or school. Furthermore, we will demonstrate how this process can help you find solutions that will remedy the situation. Finally, we will share a detailed case study showing how three sixth grade teachers and their students used *Targeted Problem-Solving* to tackle the everyday violence in their classrooms.

Part II

Thinking Through Violence Issues within *Your* School

The 3-Step Targeted Problem-Solving Process: An Overview

> *For every complex problem, there is a solution that is simple, neat, and wrong.*
>
> H. L. Mencken, newspaper columnist

Mencken, a newspaper columnist during the first half of the twentieth century, used these words to criticize the government's handling of the Depression. Today, these same words ring equally true when we consider the issues surrounding school violence. Despite the complexity of causes that explain why bullying exists, why shootings occur, or why vicious rumor mongering happens in our schools, people still search for that phantom single cause and its equally fictitious simple solution. This futile search for the simple solution leads to the kind of quick-fix efforts we cataloged in Part I—efforts that only make us feel like we're doing something, but really don't address the causes of the problem.

Many people persist in this fruitless search for the quick fix because they view problem solving as a two-step process:

1. State the problem.

2. Find a solution.

They simply state the problem and then grab at the first solution that comes to mind. This grabbing almost always results in wasted effort and resources, leaving people to wonder why the problem still persists even after they have implemented their "solution."

The focus in problem solving, however, should center on *causes*. Only after you determine the causes of a problem can you then find effective solutions that will address it. Therefore, effective problem solving includes, not two, but three, steps:

1. State the problem.

2. Determine the CAUSES.

3. Find solutions.

Effective solutions *always* connect to causes. Any school that has reduced violence did so because its solutions resolved at least one of the causes of the violence. Efforts that fail to solve the problem fall short because they miss the target; they address symptoms, not causes.

In the next three chapters, we will introduce a three-step process that can help you stay on track as you work to find effective, on-target solutions that reduce the level of violence within your school. We call this process *Targeted Problem-Solving*.

Educators in diverse settings at all grade levels across the United States have used this process successfully to tackle a myriad of complex problems within their schools. They have used the process to find effective solutions to such difficult problems as:

- low achievement in reading and mathematics,

- toxic school climates that hinder learning, and

- poor home–school relationships.

Figure II.1   Targeted Problem-Solving

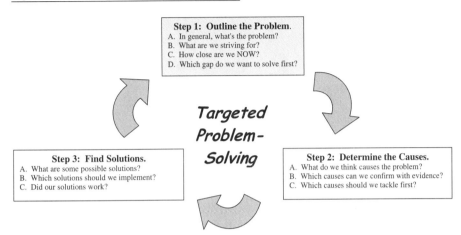

They have also used *Targeted Problem-Solving* to successfully remedy problems of violence within their schools. It is these violence issues that we have chosen to highlight in this book.

Although *Targeted Problem-Solving* works equally well regardless of the scale of violence you find yourself facing, we have elected to focus on the everyday, seemingly innocuous violence that creates an atmosphere of fear within a school. In the next three chapters, we will demonstrate how a team of middle school teachers used *Targeted Problem-Solving* to tackle the bullying and fighting happening among their students. In Part III, we give another example. This time we show how a high school confronted vicious rumor mongering among its ninth grade girls.

Even though our examples in the coming chapters will show teams of concerned adults and students using the process to address violence, *Targeted Problem-Solving* doesn't have to occur only within groups. A single teacher confronting everyday violence within his classroom can use the process with equal success. In the next three chapters, we will illustrate how Cory, a sixth grade humanities teacher, worked with two other team members to effectively deal with fights among their students. Even though Cory and his colleagues joined forces, Cory could have easily used *Targeted Problem-Solving* on his own. However, we recommend that when you do confront a problem on your own that you seek out at least one other person to serve as a sounding board. Sharing your thinking with a colleague, a trusted friend, or a handful of your students will provide you with feedback and perspectives that you cannot gain on your own.

Warning: No Quick Fixes

> *"Anything worth doing is worth doing slowly."*
>
> Gypsy Rose Lee, a famous fan dancer

As you examine Figure II.1, you will recognize that *Targeted Problem-Solving* resembles the steps in scientific inquiry. Like the scientific method, we ask that you hypothesize the causes of the problem, gather evidence to confirm or refute these hypotheses, and draw conclusions.

Unfortunately, this systematic examination of a problem goes against the grain of how people tend to do things in our society. Whenever we're faced with a problem, we immediately hear someone say: "Don't just stand there. Do something!" But that attitude often leads to wasted effort with little results. With this book, we want to change this admonishment to: "Don't just do something. Stand there. *Think* about the causes. Then do something!"

To do this, we must combat another tendency in our society— our penchant to get things done immediately. We want things solved right now, not tomorrow, but now! Regrettably, we can rarely solve complex problems so quickly. Complex problems, such as violence and bullying within our schools, require careful analysis that takes time. We have to take our cue from Gypsy Rose Lee and do it slowly, methodically, and thoroughly. Only then, do we increase our chances of actually solving the problem.

Solutions Tailored to Your School

Examining school violence slowly, methodically, and thoroughly enhances the match between your solutions and the unique context within your school. When you slow down the problem-solving process, you can focus on the particular system of causes that exist within *your* school.

Excessive speed causes people to grab at quick-fix efforts that they have seen used elsewhere. But what works in one school may not work in your school. The context within your school *is* different. Your students are different, your teachers are different, and the social norms within your school are different. Indeed, the entire environment within your school creates a unique mix of causes that requires a distinctive action plan that fits your school.

You can, of course, look to schools similar to yours for ideas on how they addressed their violence problems, but, if you want to solve your school's violence problems, you need to carefully match solutions with the causes that exist within *your* school. You must tailor your solutions to your school.

"It Takes a Village"

Earlier we suggested that the African proverb "It takes a village to raise a child" embodies a key concept of systems thinking—the interconnectedness of everyone and everything in a "village." This interconnectedness also serves as a call for all of us, no matter our roles, to take responsibility for solving the problem of violence in our school.

This responsibility also includes thinking through the problem itself. This means that all members of the school community—faculty, staff, administrators, parents, and especially students—must engage in analyzing the problem. Each member of the school community can bring to the discussion a valuable perspective about the causes of violence and possible solutions for combating that violence.

Teenagers especially can clearly articulate what's happening in a school if given the chance by adults who listen with respect, genuine concern, and without punitive judgment. Even primary students can explain to a trusted adult what happens on the schoolyard, during lunch, in the classroom, or in the bathrooms.

Including all voices within the problem-solving process not only broadens the perspectives (None of us is as smart as all of us!), but also builds ownership on the part of all members of the school community for remedying the problem. When all members of the school community—including students and their families—adopt the attitude that "it is up to us to make this work," you take a giant stride toward successfully implementing your action plan. Without this ownership in the action plan, all your careful deliberations and planning will go down the drain because you could not make your solutions happen.

The Road Ahead

In this Introduction, we've given an overview of *Targeted Problem-Solving*, with its three steps designed to lead you toward effective, on-target solutions. We warned that such deliberations may take time, but also stressed that taking a slow, methodical path will pay off in the end. Finally, we encouraged you to not go it alone as you grapple with these complex issues of violence. Rather we suggested that you include *all* voices, especially those of students and their families, in your problem-solving discussions.

For the remainder of Part II, we will give a detailed explanation of each of the three steps of *Targeted Problem-Solving*. At each point along the way, we will provide an illustration using a case study of a middle school team plagued with bullying and fights in their classrooms. Chapter 1 begins with a description of Step 1 in *Targeted Problem-Solving*, which requires that you outline the problem. With Chapter 2, we explain the all-important Step 2, where we clearly identify the causes of the problem. Chapter 3 rounds out the process with an explanation of Step 3, where we make a plan to effectively solve the problem.

Author's Note: The Genesis and Revision of *Targeted Problem–Solving*

Since its inception in 1986, I've had the privilege of working with the Accelerated Schools Project founded by Henry M. Levin, previously at Stanford University and now at Teachers' College, Columbia. I've seen school communities across the nation use the philosophy and process of Accelerated Schools to accelerate the learning of *all* their students. One of the most powerful processes within an Accelerated School is the Inquiry Process, a structured problem-solving procedure that helps teachers and administrators find solutions to the challenges they face. Building on the scientific method, the Inquiry Process uses a procedure that begins with clearly defining the core reasons *why* a problem exists.

Unfortunately, many faculties get bogged down in the Inquiry Process because they fail to sufficiently focus and narrow their problem-solving efforts *before* they begin defining why a problem exists. They simply bite off more than they can chew. My work with teachers and principals in Accelerated Schools over the years has led me to make slight modifications to the original Inquiry Process and create what I call *Targeted Problem-Solving*.

Specifically, *Targeted Problem-Solving* (Figure II.1) requires in Step 1 that problem-solvers explicitly focus and narrow their problem *before* they move into the next stages of the problem-solving process. This focusing results in making the original problem more manageable and thus more amenable to successful solutions.

Dick Lipka and I first introduced a six-step version of *Targeted Problem-Solving* in Chapter 10 of our book *Getting Answers to Your Questions: A Middle-School Educator's Guide to Program Evaluation.* Since that time, we have continued to refine the process. In this book, we introduce a version of *Targeted Problem-Solving* that combines the process into three, rather than six, easily remembered steps and incorporates an explicit systems viewpoint. We believe that you will find this new three-step version highly effective in helping you think through the violence issues within your school.

Brenda LeTendre, Co–author

Chapter 1

Step 1:
Outline the Problem

"You're just a fag!" Marshall yells as John struggles to get up. Blood oozes from John's nose. Marshall's mouth also shows a fresh wound. "Don't ever come near us again!"

Books scatter the floor around the project table and two chairs lay on their sides.

"What's going on here?" Cory Raines, the boys' sixth grade teacher, demands as he steps between the two. The whole class peers around the partition separating the Project Center from the rest of the classroom.

"Gentlemen, come with me now," Mr. Raines orders. "And the rest of you get in your seats! Now!"

Cory briskly walks the two boys down to the principal's office. His heart pumps and his mind races. He's angry. Just last week, he sent these same boys to the office two times for arguing. Apparently, the in-school suspension and loss of privileges didn't get their attention. He vows to do something about it. Things can't continue this way. He can't have any more fights in his classroom.

Introduction

Unfortunately, this scene plays out much too often in classrooms across North America. Although this type of school violence does not make the six o'clock news, it does hold the potential for escalating into the types of events we chronicled in Part I. After reviewing 37 school shootings, the U.S. Secret Service noted that the majority of the shooters had experienced persistent bullying at the hands of their classmates.[39]

Cory Raines, like teachers everywhere, knows he needs to put a stop to the fights. He knows that the fighting jeopardizes the safety and learning of not only Marshall and John, but also the other students in his class and perhaps even in the entire school. He now realizes that taking the boys to the office only serves as a stopgap measure. If he is really going to stop these fights, he must get to the roots of the problem. This is where *Targeted Problem-Solving* provides guidance.

In this chapter, we will show Cory, a sixth grade humanities teacher, and his fellow team members using Step 1 of *Targeted Problem-Solving* to outline the fighting problem they face. As we follow Cory's team through each substep, we will offer tips on how you too can use the process to tackle the violence issues you face in your classroom or school.

Figure II.2   Targeted Problem Solving

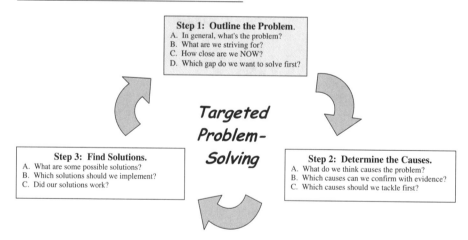

As Figure II.2 shows, *Step 1: Outline the Problem* centers around four key questions that lay the foundation for on-target, successful solutions.

A. In general, what's the problem?

B. What are we striving for?

C. How close are we NOW?

D. Which gap do we want to solve first?

Tool #1: Thinking through Violence Worksheet, found in Part IV, includes these questions along with the other guiding questions for Steps 2 and 3 of *Targeted Problem-Solving*. This quick and easy guide will walk you through each step of the process. You can also download this tool from our website at http://www.pittstate.edu/edsc/ssls/letendre.html.

Step 1: Question A— In General, What's the Problem?

As you begin Step 1 in *Targeted Problem-Solving*, you need only state the problem in very general terms. Later, you will define more specifically the problem and its root causes. Below are some examples of general problem statements:

1. Fist fights have occurred in the hallways.

2. My students bully certain students.

3. Students have an "us-against-them" attitude toward the adults in this school.

Next, you should spell out the who, what, where, and when of the problem:

Who are the perpetrators, the victims, and the bystanders? Do any patterns emerge? Do only a handful of students engage in the violent behaviors or is the problem more widespread? Does the problem exist more among younger or older students, among boys or girls?

What behaviors are the perpetrators, the victims, the bystanders, and even the adults doing during the violent incidents? Do you see any patterns in these behaviors?

Where specifically does the violence occur? Does the verbal abuse occur primarily in the cafeteria, in certain classrooms, in the hallways, in the locker rooms? Does the hostility happen in the bathrooms, at the locker areas, on the parking lot? Do students display this "us-against-them" attitude in all classrooms, in all areas of the schools or only within certain classrooms, in certain office areas?

When does the problem happen? Does the verbal abuse occur during unstructured times during the school day, during passing periods, during the lunch period, during class sessions, before or after school as students wait for busses? Does the hostility happen every day, every class period, during certain times of the year? Do students exhibit the "us-against-them" attitude when they interact with an adult privately or only when they have an audience of their peers? Do they display this attitude with all adults or only certain adults?

Finally, you also want to assess the impact the problem has on your classroom or school goals. Although your goals may vary somewhat, all schools seek to do the following:

1. Help all students achieve academically.
2. Keep students physically safe.
3. Keep students emotionally safe.
4. Retain a competent, caring, and committed staff.
5. Establish positive working relationships with families and the community.
6. Continue accreditation through government agencies or other accrediting bodies.
7. Garner sufficient funding to offer a quality educational program.
8. Maintain adequate learning facilities.

A quick assessment of the impact violence has on these eight goals helps you maintain a systems viewpoint. By making explicit the impact, you remind yourself that violence, even violence confined to just two students, often ripples through the system, affecting the academic achievement and safety of many, if not most, students. Furthermore, the violence can diminish the commitment of teachers and staff, weaken the school's relationship with families and the community, and threaten your school's accreditation and funding. Finally, violence may even result in physical damage to your school's equipment, building, or grounds.

Delineating the who, what, where, when, and impact of the violence will help you get a clearer picture of the problem you face. This clarity will serve you well when you get to Step 2 of *Targeted Problem-Solving* and begin identifying the causes of the violence within your school.

September

						1
2	3	4	5	6	7	8
9	10	11	12	13	14	15
16	17	18	19	20	21	22
23	24	25	26	27	28	29
30						

Challenge Team Example: Planning Period, Friday, September 7

It's been a rough week for Cory. On Tuesday, he hauled John and Marshall down to the office after they exchanged blows in the Project Center behind the partition in his room. The boys knocked over furniture, scattered books, and bloodied one another. Principal Miles suspended both for five days. Even in the boys' absence, the trouble continued to brew. The students just would not concentrate on their lessons. No matter what he did, they kept whispering and getting off task.

During his planning periods on Wednesday and Thursday, Cory visited individually with several students in his classes, asking them what they thought was going on between John and Marshall. He also talked with Mr. Miles, the principal; the counselor; the P.E. teacher; and the bus driver. What he learned floored him. He had no idea that Marshall teased John so much.

Cory also phoned the mothers of both boys. He still smarted from the memory of those calls. Marshall's mom sees the teasing as just a case of boys being boys, nothing more. She thinks it will blow over. She, however, was furious that Marshall was suspended over such a trivial thing and accused Cory of picking on Marshall.

John's mother blames Cory for letting all this happen. She told him that he was not doing his job, that he's not controlling his class. She even threatened that she might complain to the superintendent. She also defended John for standing up for himself. "No one else defends him, so I told him he has to do it himself," she said as she hung up the phone.

At the Challenge Team's Friday planning session, Cory described his week to his fellow team members Joan Stark and Mellie Arevalos.

"What can I do?" Cory asked. "I can't endure another week like this," he sighed with exasperation.

"It's more like what can *we* do?" Joan answered. "You're not the only one having a problem. In my class it's not Marshall and John, it's Tony and John. They haven't come to blows yet, but I see the signs."

"You're right," Mellie added. "I think this goes beyond Marshall and John. We need to do something starting next week or we'll be talking about this problem for the rest of the year."

"OK, so what do we do?" Cory asked.

"During the summer I attended one of those short courses at the university and the instructor shared a process she called *Targeted Problem-Solving*," Joan replied. "She even gave us a website with resources for using the process. I think I still have my notes in the file cabinet. I think this process is just what we need to get this mess stopped."

Joan searched through her file cabinet and found her notes from the course. The trio went on-line to http://www.pittstate.edu/edsc/ssls/letendre.html and downloaded a copy of Tool #1: Thinking Through Violence Worksheet. Joan briefly explained each step to her colleagues and they decided to fill out the form on-screen.

"Well, the answer to Step 1, Question A seems pretty straightforward, don't you think?" Cory asked rhetorically as he typed:

```
We have shouting matches and fights happening
among students on the Challenge Team.
```

Joan and Mellie nodded in agreement.

"Now we need to go into more detail," Joan said as she pointed to the blank boxes on the computer screen.

Cory's fingers paused at the keyboard as the group members discussed how they wanted to complete the rest of Question A. After 15 minutes, the group's digital worksheet looked like Figure II.3.

Figure II.3   Tool #1: Thinking through Violence Worksheet

Step 1: Outline the Problem

A. In general, what's the problem?
We have shouting matches and fights happening among students on the Challenge Team.

Who (Perpetrators? Victims? By-standers? Any patterns?)	• Marshall and John -- 2 shouting matches, 1 fight • Marshall teasing John about being "queer" • Tony teasing John • Almost all of the students "rubberneck" and gather around.
What (Behaviors of perpetrators, victims, by-standers, adults. Any patterns?)	• Marshall picking on, teasing John about being "queer" • Cory separated John and Marshall, dispersed the on-lookers, immediately wrote out a disciplinary referral, marked a disciplinary demerit for both boys, took them to the principal's office (after calling ahead to alert the office). • Principal assigned each boy 3 days in-school suspension for the shouting matches and 5 days out-of-school suspension for the fighting. • Marshall quietly starts publicly teasing John and then increases it until John can't stand it any more and yells "Stop it! Then the teasing continues loudly with name-calling and obscenities, all designed to get John to do more shouting and eventually get him in trouble. • Tony and John arguing in Joan's classroom before and after class. Sometimes during class but Joan has separated the boys and that seems to stop their angry whispers. • Mellie hasn't seen any disturbances between John and other students during math class, although John purposely sits in the desk away from all the other students except for Twyla who appears to be John's friend. • During fight/argument, other students "rubberneck," some inciting the boys to fight. • No students try to calm the situation down.
Where (Physical location of the incidents. Patterns?)	• Fight occurred in the Project Center behind the partition in Cory's classroom. • The shouting matches between Marshall and John happened in the hallway by Cory's door. • Marshall teases John in lunchroom, in the hallways, in P.E. class, on the bus.
When (Timing of the incidents. Any patterns? Frequency)	• Fight occurred during p.m. free reading time right after lunch. • Shouting matches occurred as students returned from P.E. class before Cory's class began. • Teasing of John happens daily during lunch and on the bus, periodically during unstructured class time.

Impact on school's overall goals

Academic Achievement	• Causes loss of instructional time for all students. • John, Marshall, and Tony can't learn when their emotions are flaring. John, particularly, afraid of what will happen to him and whether his grades will go down. • For the hour of class time following a shouting match, all students, even those who only observed the shouting match, have a hard time focusing on the lesson. It clouds the entire learning climate.
Physical safety	Potential for more fights.
Emotional safety	Students afraid they may be next.
Staff	Taking much of Cory's time. Stress on all three of us.
Parents/Community	Cory had some very distraught phone calls from John's parents. John's mother, particularly, blames Cory for what's happening. Marshall's mom thinks Cory's picking on him and sending him to the office for "boys being boys."
Accreditation	N/A
Funding	N/A
Facilities/Maintenance	N/A

Step 1: Question B—
What are We Striving For?

Labeling situations as problems requires that you have an ideal situation already in mind. When you compare "what is" to "what should be," you see a glaring gap and call this a problem. Regrettably, too often the ideal situation we have in mind is implicit, unspoken, and even quite fuzzy. By answering Step 1, Question B, you make explicit how your ideal situation will look. Later, you will take stock of just how close you are *now* to this vision and this comparison will help you identify where you need to start in solving your problem.

In answering the question "What are we striving for?" your portrait of the ideal situation should refrain from describing *how* you will solve the problem. Rather, you should focus on specifying the behavioral outcomes for both students and adults.

For example, let's say that part of a school's vision of a safe learning environment includes the statement:

We are striving for students to use the XYZ Conflict Resolution Program. This statement is really a *solution*. A more appropriate answer to *"What are we striving for?"* is this: *We want our students to resolve conflicts in a productive manner, without resorting to verbal or physical violence.*

Notice that this vision does not give any hint as to *how* you will solve the problem, but it does clearly define what you're striving for. This clear definition of what you want serves as the foundation for Question C within Step 1: *"How close are we NOW?"* In this substep, you will take stock of each component of your safe school vision to see just how close you are now to achieving that outcome.

From your general vision statement, you then need to specify outcomes for both students and adults. For example, from the above vision statement we might generate the following outcomes:

> Outcome 1:   Students will resolve conflicts in a productive manner.

Outcome 2:   All school adults will encourage students to resolve conflicts in a productive manner.

Outcome 3:   Parents/family members will encourage students to resolve conflicts in a productive manner.

Call Upon Many Voices

As you delineate what your safe learning environment would look like, we encourage you to seek input from many voices. Ask the adults and students alike: "What would a safe school look like? What would a safe classroom look like?" If you are tackling a schoolwide violence issue, we suggest that you ask both the adults that work within the school and those in the community who have a stake in the school's safety—families of the students, members of the police and fire departments, medical professionals, and other concerned citizens.

Building consensus around a vision of a safe learning environment lays a solid foundation for the successful implementation of the solutions you eventually will devise. First, it builds ownership among the students and the adults for the violence problem itself, and once people "own" a problem, they become much more committed to doing something to solve that problem.

Second, delineating a shared vision engenders among members of the school community a sense of possibility that they can indeed achieve a physically and emotionally safe learning environment. In many school settings, the adults and students alike have been lulled into accepting violence as a fact of life that won't change. To alter this attitude, three things must happen:

1. People must feel a shared dissatisfaction with the way things currently stand. They must come to say with conviction: "We won't stand for this anymore!"

2. They must believe that they can actually do something about the problem. They must see that they have the will, resources, skills, time, and energy to make the changes.

3. Finally, they must share in a vision of where they want to go. They must know what they're striving for.

The process of forging a vision of a safe learning environment fulfills all three of these required elements and puts your school on a track toward successful change. Stephen Covey reminds us that talking about methods creates division within a group, but talking about goals builds agreement.[40] Forging a vision of a safe school or classroom starts to build that agreement.

Other Relevant Voices

Besides the opinions of those within your school community, you may also want to consult sources within the educational literature that can give you some ideas of what a physically and emotionally safe school environment looks like. At our website (http:/ /www.pittstate.edu/edsc/ssls/letendre.html) we provide annotations of both print and Internet resources that can help you generate ideas about your vision of a safe school.

Refrain from Using a "Canned" Vision

To save time, some people may simply pick up a safe school vision from another school. However, we suggest that you not do this. The power of a safe school vision lies primarily in the *process* of forging that vision. While crafting a vision statement, people engage in valuable discussions and reflection, both of which help build their ownership in the vision itself and a commitment to making that vision a reality within their school and classrooms. Simply handing people a "canned" statement pulled off the Internet from another school bypasses this crucial process of forging the vision. They never own the vision and thus rarely commit to it.

However, we don't want to leave you with the impression that you must craft your vision from scratch. You definitely want to begin by asking members of the school community the open-ended questions: "In your opinion, what does a safe school look like? What does a safe classroom look like?" But once you get their creative juices flowing, you can stimulate them even more by showing them what other schools have written and what researchers and experts say. Your eventual vision of a safe school could easily reflect a balance of both—what's in *your* hearts and minds and what others have done.

September						
						1
2	3	4	5	6	7	8
9	10	11	12	13	14	15
16	17	18	19	20	21	22
23	24	25	26	27	28	29
30						

Challenge Team Example: Planning Period, Friday, September 7, Continued

"Now that we've described our problem and its impact, we need to decide just what we're striving for," Joan emphasized as she pointd to the blank outcome boxes on the Thinking Through Violence Worksheet.

"I think that's also pretty straightforward, as well," Cory suggested. "We want the fighting to stop."

"Yes, that's right," Mellie agreed. "However, I think we really want more. I believe we want a safe learning environment not just for John, but for all the students."

Cory and Joan nodded.

"So, what should I type in these boxes for outcomes?" Cory asked.

The team continued their discussion as Cory typed their list of outcomes into the form.

After about five minutes, Mellie spoke up.

"It just occurred to me that we're forgetting some very important people in all this discussion," she mused. "Here we are talking about what *we* are striving for. That's fine, but we should also get ideas from the students themselves. If we're really serious about solving this fighting problem, we need to get the students involved. We can't do this alone. We need their help. If they see it as their responsibility, along with ours, to stop this fighting, then we can solve this problem. I suggest that we put our ideas down today, but next week we need talk with the students in our classes and get their views."

"I could do that on Tuesday and Wednesday in my classes," Cory volunteered. "Seems like a natural thing since the fight occurred in my classroom. Plus we could get John and Marshall's ideas as well. They'll be back from their suspension on Wednesday. I don't know if I'll get much from the two of them, but I'll try."

"Why don't you let me visit with each of them privately?" Mellie offered. "John particularly seems fairly comfortable talking with me."

"Fine, that's sounds like a good idea," replied Cory.

"What about the parents? Shouldn't we get their input as well?" Joan wondered.

"Sure, but how do you suggest that we do that?" asked Mellie.

"Well, perhaps I can have the students interview their parents as a homework assignment," Cory suggested. "We're working on questioning as a way to gather data and this would fit right in with my current unit in social studies."

"OK, so on Tuesday and Wednesday you'll get the students' ideas and on Thursday you'll have the parents' ideas," Joan reviewed the group's decision. "Then Friday at our planning time, we can add all their ideas to this worksheet."

"So what do we have down so far?" Mellie asked as she peered at the computer screen.

Figure II.4   Challenge Team's Tool #1, Step B

Step 1: Outline the Problem

B. What outcomes are we striving for?

Student behavior outcomes?	John and Marshall will not fight. Marshall and Tony will stop teasing John. Other students won't condone teasing. Students will not incite John and Marshall to fight.
Teacher/staff behavior outcomes?	We will handle these misbehaviors in our own class and not send the offenders to the office unless they fight. We will create an emotionally safe learning environment for all students. We will create a physically safe learning environment for all students.
Parent/Family, Community behavior outcomes?	Marshall's mom will support us in our efforts to get Marshall to behave.

Step 1: Question C— How Close Are We NOW?

At this point in *Targeted Problem-Solving*, you have stated your problem in general terms and delineated what you are striving for. Question C now asks you to take stock of your vision and answer the question: "How close are we NOW?" This taking stock serves multiple purposes:

a. To help identify what's going *wrong* to help you distinguish symptoms from root causes,

b. To recognize what's going *right* so you will know the strengths you can build on when you design your solutions, and

c. To gather baseline data so that you will have a reference point when you later ask: "Did our solutions work?"

Obtaining Evidence

Taking stock requires that you use evidence, not speculation, to make judgments about how close you are to achieving your vision of a safe learning environment. So what constitutes evidence? In a court of law, evidence consists of "the data, in the form of testimony of witnesses, documents or other objects (such as a photograph, a revolver, etc.) identified by witnesses, offered to the court or jury in proof of the facts in issue."[41] The same definition holds for *Targeted Problem-Solving*. Notice the key words in the preceding definition: "data" and "proof of the facts." There's no room for gut feelings. *Targeted Problem-Solving* requires that you move away from conjecture and instead look at the facts and draw reasonable conclusions from those facts.

In some cases, you might already have solid evidence to help you decide how close you are to achieving your vision of a safe school. Schools abound with all sorts of data collected daily as a matter of course. For example, your school profile created as part of a school improvement plan often summarizes key measures of your school's progress in the area of student behavior. Furthermore, the principal's office maintains a record of every discipline referral made by teachers, every disciplinary letter sent to parents, and every assignment to in-school or out-of-school suspension. The office also keeps attendance and tardy data, standardized testing data, and some offices even maintain a log of all incoming and outgoing phone calls. Finally, teachers' grade books include evidence about student achievement and behavior.

If you don't have the evidence already in hand, you will need to collect the data using three basic methods:

>   a.   Asking people for information and perceptions through surveys or interviews,

>   b.   Observing situations, and

>   c.   Reviewing documents.

Although entire graduate courses and methods of research texts address the issues involved in collecting data, *Targeting Problem-Solving* does not require that you conduct a doctoral dissertation to get the evidence you need. However, you should gather your data in an objective and systematic manner.

By objective, we mean that you should use methods that minimize bias as much as possible. How can you do this?

First, you can continually ask yourself: *"Will these data look credible in the eyes of others?"* and plan accordingly.

Second, you can collect data from different sources (e.g., teachers, administrators, students) using different methods (e.g., review of documents, interviews with parents, classroom observations). If all the data point one way, you can feel reasonably sure that you have a true picture of the situation.

Third, you can carefully craft surveys that refrain from asking questions that may lead people to answer in socially desirable ways rather than how they really see things. For example, rather than asking students "Do *you* try to get people to fight when you see them arguing?" ask them to describe what bystanders tend to do while watching arguments or fights.

Finally, you can ask open-ended questions that give people wide latitude for answers.

For further guidance on how to gather credible data, we invite you to visit our website (http://www.pittstate.edu/edsc/ssls/letendre.html) that supports our previous two books: *An Elementary Educator's Guide to Evaluation* and *Getting Answers to Your Questions: A Middle School Educator's Guide to Program Evaluation.* A click on the book titles will take you to the buttons for "Recommended Books" and "Recommended Sites." Here, you will find annotations and links to resources that can guide you in your data collection efforts.

Making Judgments

Once you have your evidence in hand, we suggest that you use the Taking Stock Matrix in Figure II.5 to guide you in making judgments about each component of your safe school vision. (Note: You will find a blank copy of Tool #2 in the Tool Kit, Part IV. Also you can visit our website at http://www.pittstate.edu/edsc/ssls/letendre.html and download the form.) In Column A of the Taking Stock Matrix, you list each component of the safe school vision you delineated in answering Question B: What are we striving for?

Figure II.5   Tool #2: Taking Stock Matrix

How close are we NOW to achieving our outcomes?						
Column A: Safe School Vision Components	No where near				Fully achieved	Column B Supporting Evidence??
	0	**1**	**2**	**3**	**4**	**5**	

Then using evidence, you make a judgment as to how close you are *now* to achieving each component. The form uses a scale from 0 to 5, with "0" meaning that you have achieved no progress on this particular component, either because you have not yet tried to address this piece or you tried and failed. You would award a score of "5" to any vision component that you have *fully* achieved. For pieces of your vision on which you have made some progress, you would assign a "1," "2," "3," or "4" depending on how close you are to fully achieving them.

Also notice that Tool #2 asks you to summarize in Column B the evidence that supports your judgment for that vision component. This column helps you remember that you should base your judgments on data and not speculation.

Once you have taken stock using Tool #2 (see Figure II.5) you can easily scan the form and summarize both the gaps you need to address, as well as the strengths you can build upon as you design your solutions. Outcomes receiving a rating of less than "5" show gaps. Later you will use this information to decide which of these gaps to address first. Outcomes with "5's" indicate strengths and even those with ratings of "3" and "4" point to relative strengths.

We strongly suggest that you explicitly identify the strengths. Even the most violence-ridden school has some strengths going for it. Later, in Step 3, when you begin crafting your solutions you will find that these strengths can form a solid foundation on which you can successfully build your interventions.

September						
						1
2	3	4	5	6	7	8
9	10	11	12	13	14	15
16	17	18	19	20	21	22
23	24	25	26	27	28	29
30						

Challenge Team Example: Planning Period, Friday, September 7, Continued

"We've got about 20 minutes until the students come in. Can we start taking stock even though we don't yet have the students' and parents' ideas on the vision?" Joan asked.

"Sure, let's start with what we have and then revisit it next Friday during our planning time after we hear what the students and their families have to say," Cory answered.

Cory typed in the team's vision components and the three worked their way down the form, judging the current status of each vision piece. To make their judgments, they drew on their own observations over the past weeks, reviewed the merit/demerit logs they kept as part of the team's discipline plan, and discussed the conversations Cory had with the students, Principal Miles, the counselor, the P.E. teacher, the bus driver, and the mothers of both John and Marshall.

Just as the students filed into the room, Cory saved the Taking Stock Matrix shown in Figure II.6. He quickly sent the

Figure II.6   Tool #2: Taking Stock Matrix Created by the Challenge Team Teachers

| Step 1: Outline the Problem |

C. How close are we NOW?

How close are we NOW to achieving our outcomes?							
Column A: What I am striving for?	No where near					Fully achieved	Column B: Supporting Evidence??
	0	**1**	**2**	**3**	**4**	**5**	
John and Marshall will not fight.	X						• Our observations • Cory's conversation with Principal Miles
Marshall and Tony will stop teasing John	X						• Our observations • Demerit logs • Conversations with students, staff
Other students won't condone teasing.			X				• Conversations with students • Demerit logs • Our observations
Students will not incite John and Marshall to fight.				X		Sara Julie Mark	• Demerit logs • Our observations
We will handle these misbehaviors in our own classes and not send the offenders to the office unless they fight.		X					• Review of our handling of incidents
We will create an emotionally safe learning environment for all students.	John	Marshall & Tony	X				• Our observations • Conversations with students
We will create a physically safe learning environment for all students.	John Marshall Tony	X					• Our observations • Conversations with students
Marshall's mom will support us in our efforts to get Marshall to behave.	X						• Cory's conversations with Marshall and his mom

document to the printer and made three copies, one for each member of the team. The teachers gathered up their materials and hurried to meet their students for the last period of the day.

Step 1: Question D— Which Gap Do We Solve First?

As you scan your completed Taking Stock Matrix (similar to Figure II.6), you will most likely find not just one gap, but many gaps. Now you face the quandary of where to begin. You could, of course, try to address all these gaps simultaneously. However, we suggest that you not do this. You would spread yourself and your colleagues too thin and find that you accomplish very little. Rather, we encourage you to focus on resolving one or two of the gaps and then later return to your list of gaps and systematically address the others. Our experience has shown us that focusing attention on a handful of carefully selected gaps will actually resolve most of the gaps on your list.

But the question still remains: "Which of these gaps do you tackle first?" We suggest that you take one of three pathways:

1. Tackle the gap that will give you the biggest impact for your effort.

    In other words, which gap, if you could close it/ solve it, would also close other gaps? For example, a group of middle school teachers dealing with excessive shouting matches in the cafeteria found that their taking stock evidence showed that few students knew how to resolve conflicts in a productive manner. The teachers decided that if students learned conflict-resolution skills and used those skills, then the shouting matches would subside. Furthermore, they reasoned that a number of other problems around the school would also dissipate. Thus, the team of teachers decided definitely to move this gap to the solution step.

2. Begin with an outcome that received a "3" or "4" rating and would take only a bit of concerted effort to get to a "5."

> Starting with a more easily solved gap can give you some initial success and get the momentum started toward solving the violence issues within your school. "Let's start with something easy and then move on to the harder stuff" does make sense. However, we want to strongly urge you to also tackle the hard stuff as soon as you can. If you don't, you will never really resolve your violence problem.

3. Begin with an outcome that combines high impact with a foundation of strength.

> Thus, you may want to move high impact outcomes that you rated as relative strengths ("3" or "4") to the solution stage of *Targeted Problem-Solving.*

Sometimes deciding which gap you want to solve first can bring out the fireworks in a group as people voice their different opinions. People will often feel strongly about following one of the three paths we outlined above. We suggest that you not let these differences in opinions bog you down. Rather build consensus among your group about the most plausible starting point. Sometimes you can compromise and tackle two or three gaps at a time. Also, you can remind people that you will eventually cycle back and resolve all the gaps on your list.

September						
						1
2	3	4	5	6	7	8
9	10	11	12	13	14	15
16	17	18	19	20	21	22
23	24	25	26	27	28	29
30						

Challenge Team Example: Planning Period, Friday, September 14

"Wow! What a week," Mellie exclaimed as she took her usual seat at the round conference table in Cory's classroom. "The kids are really buzzing about the discussions you've been having with them, Cory. They want to stop the fighting and teasing as much as we do. They've really taken this seriously. Or at least most of them have. Tiffany and her bunch are still hanging back, but I get the sense that they'll come around soon. Tiffany can't stand being out of step."

"Yeah," Joan agreed. "Tiffany wants to be out in front, leading. I'm amazed how she has that group of boys wrapped around her finger. Marshall, Tony, and Stan will do just about anything to get her attention. And Sharon and Christina hang on her every word. Perhaps we can now channel Tiffany's natural leadership abilities into something more positive."

"So, Cory, let's hear how it went," Mellie leaned forward, focusing her full attention on Cory. "What did the students have to say? What about their parents?"

Cory gave a quick review of the discussions in his classes. On Tuesday before John and Marshall returned from suspension, Cory spent a major part of his class time talking with the students about the teasing problem. He explained to the classes that the teasing went beyond one or two people, that it was happening much too often in all classes.

"At first it was slow going," Cory explained. "The students seemed afraid to talk about it but Allison spoke up and got the ball rolling. Everyone seems to really respect what she has to say. Then the most amazing thing happened. When I asked them to brainstorm what we should be striving for, they came up with essentially the very same things we mentioned last Friday during our planning session. We're more together on this than I initially thought."

Mellie smiled. "Seems that all we have to do is give them a chance and they'll rise to the occasion."

"And they certainly did. They even suggested some things that we didn't think about," Cory continued. "They want everyone to stop teasing, not just Marshall and Tony to stop. Also, last Friday when we listed our outcomes for the parents, we simply stated that we wanted Marshall's mom to support us. Well, the students think we should want all their families to support us. And the parent interviews show that the families indeed want to help us stop all this teasing and fighting."

Mellie smiled even more broadly. "So it looks like we need to add that to our outcomes section."

"And we also need to indicate on our Taking Stock Matrix that we have a strength when it comes to potential support from the parents," Joan added, as she opened the digital copy of the Thinking Through Violence Worksheet and made the changes.

"So how did John and Marshall react to all of this when they returned on Wednesday?" Joan inquired.

"At first things were a bit rocky," Cory acknowledged. "When the boys returned on Wednesday, the students excitedly told them about our discussions of the teasing and fighting. Both boys eyed each other and their classmates cautiously," Cory continued. "For the next few days, the two boys stepped around each other gingerly. A couple of times Marshall started chanting under his breathe 'fag, fag, fag' at John, but the students sitting next to Marshall eyed him with disapproval. Even Tiffany called him a 'baby.'"

"You know what, I think we've turned a corner on this problem and we haven't even started thinking about solutions yet," Mellie commented.

"I agree," Joan said, "but we still have lots of work to do before we really solve this problem. Every outcome on our Taking Stock Matrix shows a gap. We can't address all of them right now. That would swamp us. I suggest that we look over the matrix and decide which gap we want to tackle first."

As they scan their Taking Stock Matrix, the trio asked two questions:

- Which gap, if we could solve it, would also close other gaps?
- Which outcomes would require only a bit of concerted effort to get to a "5," fully achieved rating?

After much discussion, the trio designated the following as high priority gaps:

- We need the teasing to stop, particular the teasing of John by Marshall and Tony.
- We need to create an emotionally safe learning environment for all students.
- We need to create a physically safe learning environment for all students.

The team felt they must give immediate attention to the teasing. Furthermore, they realized that by getting the teasing stopped, they would take a major step toward closing the other two priority gaps. Creating emotionally and physically safe classrooms would boost student learning and certainly had ramifications beyond the current troubles.

As Joan types their priority gaps into the digital worksheet, Mellie glanced at the clock.

"We have only five minutes until the kids get back," she announced. "I don't think we can wait until next Friday to work on this again. I know Monday's an individual planning day, but could we do a team meeting instead?"

"Definitely," Cory and Joan concurred.

"Plus, I would like to take the next step in my discussions with the students," Cory continued. "Monday, I want to get their ideas about possible causes for all this teasing. Also I would like to try this cause-mapping process that you told us about last week."

"Great idea," Joan commended. "That means when we get into hypothesizing possible causes we will have their ideas and ours."

"OK, it's a plan. We meet Monday. How about in my class-room?" Mellie suggested.

The Road Ahead

At this point in *Targeted Problem-Solving*, Cory and his team have completed Step 1 and answered four key questions:

A. In general, what's the problem?

B. What are we striving for?

C. How close are we NOW?

D. Which gap do we want to solve first?

In Chapter Two, we now move to the most crucial step in the process—identifying the causes of the violence problem. To augment our explanation, we will continue to show how Cory and his colleagues analyze the teasing and fighting problem among their students.

Chapter 2

Step 2:
Determine the Causes

"A problem well put is a problem half solved."

John Dewey, Educator

Introduction

Thus far in our search for solutions, we have:

1. Stated the problem in very general terms,

2. Described what we are striving for,

3. Taken stock of how close we now are to our ideal situation, and

4. Decided which of the gaps we want to solve first.

Now, we come to an absolutely crucial stage in *Targeted Problem-Solving*—defining the causes of the problem. Unfortunately, most people, including educators, often skip this step. They simply leap at the first solution that occurs to them, even if that solution will not come close to addressing the violence problem. Our culture is so bent toward action that when we see a problem we just act, often wasting time, money, and energy on nonsolutions that miss the target. If you truly want to lower the level of violence within your school, you must identify and address the underlying causes of this violence. In Step 2 of *Targeted Problem-Solving* we avoid gut-level thinking and instead conduct a strict cause-and-effect analysis supported with evidence.

In this chapter, we will walk through this critical Step 2: Determine the Causes. We will continue to clarify each point along with way with the work of Cory and his fellow team members as they tackle the teasing and fighting among their students.

Figure II.7   Targeted Problem-Solving

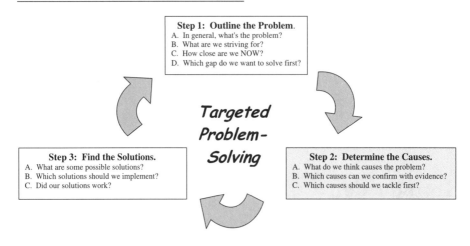

As Figure II.7 shows, Step 2 centers around three key questions that lay the foundation for on-target, successful solutions

A. What do we think causes the problem?

B. Which causes can we confirm with evidence?

C. Which causes should we tackle first?

To guide you in using *Targeted Problem-Solving*, you can again turn to Tool #1 of the Tool Kit in Part IV. This worksheet also makes a good note-taking device, helping you keep track of your deliberations. We suggest that you either photocopy Tool #1 or download it from our website at http://www.pittstate.edu/edsc/ssls/letendre.html.

Step 2: Question A— What Do We Think Causes the Problem?

Unfortunately, we humans are prone to seeing things one way, our way, too often closing our minds to other possibilities. Indeed, when it comes to problem solving, we tend to "think" with our gut feelings rather than our brains. We often settle on the first cause that occurs to us, saying, "I know what's causing the problem. It's plain as day!" and then immediately shut our minds to other possibilities. Regrettably, these gut feelings often center on symptoms rather than root causes. Question A of Step 2, however, pushes us to look beyond the single, phantom cause and, instead, identify the *system of causes* that contributes to the violence problems we face.

Seek Multiple Viewpoints

To ensure that you consider all possible reasons why a violence problem exists in your school rather than just the "pet theories" of a few, we suggest that you go to a wide range of people and ask the same question: *What do you think causes the problem?*

Indeed, we suggest that you seek viewpoints from the following groups:

(a) Students from all different subgroups within your school.

> This includes members of the various cliques, along with victims, perpetrators, and on-lookers of violent acts.

(b) Teachers.

(c) Staff members such as secretaries, janitors, bus drivers, instructional aides, and food-service workers.

Because they observe students interacting in unstructured settings, these staff members often see and hear things that teachers and principals rarely witness.

(d) Principal and vice-principals.

(e) Parents and guardians of students from the different subgroups we listed in letter "a."

(f) School counselors.

(g) Others within your community who work with young people such as pastors, police officers, juvenile justice officials, and directors of after-school youth programs (e.g., Boys and Girls Club, the "Y," sports leagues).

We also suggest that you consult the educational literature, examining what experts and researchers have to say about the causes of the violence within schools. On our website at http://www.pittstate.edu/edsc/ssls/letendre.html, we give annotations for resources that report key research findings.

Finally, you should review relevant documents (such as disciplinary referrals), make observations, and examine your taking-stock information, all the while asking: *What do we think causes the problem?*" Often reexamining such evidence will help you see additional causes that you previously overlooked.

Hypothesizing About Causes

All successful problem solving rests on a foundation of hypotheses—educated guesses about what causes the problem. As you ask people within the school, "What do you think causes the problem?" you will find that they will often cite causes emphatically, saying "The cause of the problem is...." But your job is to see these emphatic statements instead as hypotheses that require confirmation with evidence. Without supporting evidence, these cause statements are simply speculation.

At this point in Step 2, you should brainstorm freely, generating as many hypotheses as you can. Later, you will remove the duplicates and use evidence to see whether or not these hypothesized causes actually hold up under scrutiny.

Zooming In and Zooming Out to Identify Causes

We've already suggested that you begin hypothesizing possible causes by asking a wide variety of people what they think causes the problem. However, even though you cast your net wide and query many people, you may not get the full range of possible causes. This is where systems thinking can help. In Part I, we introduced you to the concept of systems thinking and urged you to view your school as a multi-layered set of parts that interact and work as a whole. By examining each level, you can often generate additional hypotheses about the causes of the violence problem.

Figure II.8   The System and Subsystems in a School

School
Grade Levels
Classrooms
Teacher-Students
Student Subgroups
Individual Student

For example, Figure II.8 shows a portion of the subsystems a typical school, moving from the whole to smaller and smaller subsystems, from the entire school to the individual students. By zooming in (taking the micro view) and zooming out (taking the macro view) through the various levels, you can examine the violence problem from various perspectives and generate additional, and often less obvious, possible causes. Figure II.9 shows examples of questions that you might ask as you zoom in and zoom out during your analysis.

Figure II.9   Zooming In and Zooming Out to Analyze Violence

Zooming Out—The MACRO View

Is something about the discipline policies that govern our **entire school** causing the problem? For example, does our school-wide rules about fighting contribute to the problem?

Is something about the discipline policies that govern this **particular grade level** causing the problem? For example, do the rules about fighting used by the teachers at this grade level contribute to the problem?

Is something about the discipline policies within this **particular classroom** causing the problem? For example, do the rules about fighting used by <u>this</u> teacher contribute to the problem?

Is something about the discipline policies within this particular classroom as applied to a **certain subgroup** of students causing the problem? For example, does this teacher treat girls differently than boys when it comes to the rules about fighting?

Is something about the discipline policies within this particular classroom as applied to a **specific student** causing the problem? For example, does this teacher treat Angela differently than the other girls when it comes to the rules about fighting?

Zooming In—The MICRO View

Other types of questions can also help as you zoom in and out of the various subsystems. For example:

- Is there any thing about our *curriculum* that might be causing the problem?

- Is there any thing about our *instructional strategies* that might be causing the problem?

- Is there any thing about how *we organize for learning* that might be causing the problem? For example, is there any thing about how we organize classrooms, assign students to specific classrooms, or divide up the learning time during the day that might be causing the problem?

- Is there any thing about our *procedures* that might be causing the problem?

- Is there any thing about our *policies* that might be causing the problem?

Tool # 1: Thinking Through Violence Worksheet includes a list of guiding questions that can help you expand your thinking about the possible causes of your school's violence issues.

Digging Even Deeper

As you review the hypotheses you've generated, you may find that you need to dig even deeper, breaking down general hypotheses into more specific ones. For example, let's say the general problem we're addressing is:

> "Students engage in verbal harassment during passing periods."

Someone offers this hypothesis:

> "Students engage in verbal harassment because they're frustrated."

We need to dig deeper with this hypothesis, asking: *Why are students frustrated?* This question then yields further hypotheses:

- Because they are not clear about what they are expected to do in their classes.

- Because the tasks they face in class are too challenging or not challenging enough.

- Because they have no voice or choice in the kinds of learning experiences they have in their classes.

- Because they do not feel cared for or respected as a person by their classmates, teachers, or administrators.

And, of course, you can dig even deeper by asking another round of "why" questions:

- Why are students not clear on what is expected of them?
- Why do students find the tasks too challenging? Not challenging enough?
- Why do students have no voice?
- Why do students feel like they aren't cared for? Respected?

"This is SO Complex My Head Hurts!"

As you analyze a complex problem, like fighting within your school, you will most likely identify scores of possible causes as to why the fighting occurs. You may find the complexity of causes intimidating—so overwhelming that you want to throw up your hands in disgust.

But we beg you to hang in there. You will find that this careful analysis at the various levels of the system *will* yield a set of manageable causes at each level (schoolwide, grade-level, Ms. Brown's classroom). Later in Step 3, you and your colleagues can craft a coordinated action plan that addresses the causes at all levels, with people at each level within the school doing their part to help solve the problem.

Cause Mapping

At this point in Step 2 of *Targeted Problem-Solving,* you may have as many as 30 to 40 hypothesized causes of the violence problem you face. Now you need to organize all these educated guesses so that you and your colleagues can get a handle on these causes. To do this, we recommend that you use a technique known as cause mapping. With this tool, you create a visual picture, a map, that summarizes all your hypotheses into clusters of cause-and-effect relationships. The cause map provides you with a view of all the possible causes for your particular violence problem.

You've already seen an example of cause mapping at work. Earlier in Part I, we used the example of a car accident on a rainy night to illustrate the concept that an event occurs not because of one cause, but because of a system of causes. We provided the graphic you see in Figure II.10 to display this system of causes for the car accident. This graphic is a rudimentary cause map.

A cause map begins with the resulting incident and then backward maps the system of causes that contributed to that incident. A full-blown cause map displays not only the cause–effect relationships, but also includes a brief statement of the evidence that confirms each cause. In this way, you can stay true to the dictum for successful problem solving offered by Dragnet's Detective Sergeant Joe Friday: "Just the facts, ma'am. Nothing but the facts!"

A cause map not only serves to summarize your thinking about the cause–effect relationships that contribute to the violence issues in your school, but it can also jump start further insights into the problem itself. Essentially, as you create a cause map, you and your colleagues will engage in further discussions, digging deeper into possible causes and identifying additional possible causes. Plus, you will begin to see the less obvious connections among factors. All this can lead you to new insights that will ultimately result in more effective solutions to your violence problem.

Rather than get into the details of how to create a cause map here, we believe a good example is worth a 1000 words. Therefore, later in this section, we will illustrate how Cory, Joan, and Mellie use cause mapping to analyze the teasing and fighting among their students. Also Tool #3 in the Tool Kit gives a "how-to" lesson in cause mapping, complete with do's and don'ts.

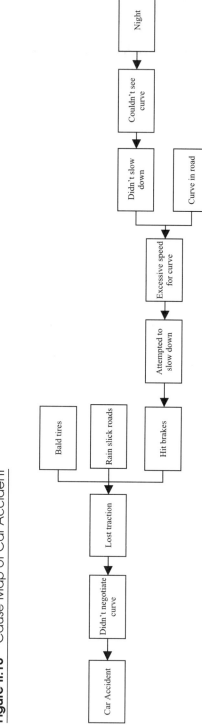

Figure II.10   Cause Map of Car Accident

Creating a Group Memory

Part of the power of cause mapping lies in its ability to visually capture the sum of your group's knowledge and understanding of the problem. This visual documentation of your deliberations can serve you in three ways. First, it can prevent you from having to spend precious time and effort rehashing previous discussions. Rarely can you fully analyze a complex violence issue in one meeting. Such problems require several meetings involving many people. A cause map creates a memory of your discussions so that at each new meeting, you can turn to your cause map and pick up where you left off, rather than covering the same ground over and over.

Second, a cause map makes it easy to pull in new people, with fresh perspectives, to your discussions. A cause map communicates your thinking in such a way that others, who have not participated in the initial discussions, can readily comprehend what you have done and how you think about the problem. These new people can jump right into your discussions after only a brief orientation.

Finally, a visual cause map can help in future problem solving. The cause map represents a concise, easily understood documentation of your analysis on the current problem. In the future, should you or others in your school face a similar problem, you don't have to start from scratch. You can pull out your previous cause map and use it as a springboard for your new analyses.

September						
						1
2	3	4	5	6	7	8
9	10	11	12	13	14	15
16	17	18	19	20	21	22
23	24	25	26	27	28	29
30						

Challenge Team Example: Over the Weekend

Right after John and Marshall returned from their five-day suspension for fighting, Mellie had taken each of the boys aside privately and talked with them about the fighting and teasing. She wanted to hear their sides of the story. After some initial hesitancy, both boys opened up to her and candidly answered her questions. At yesterday's planning session, the team decided to focus on finding solutions to the teasing problem in general. Mellie definitely agreed that

Figure II.11   Portion of Mellie's Cause Map for the Fight Between Marshall and John

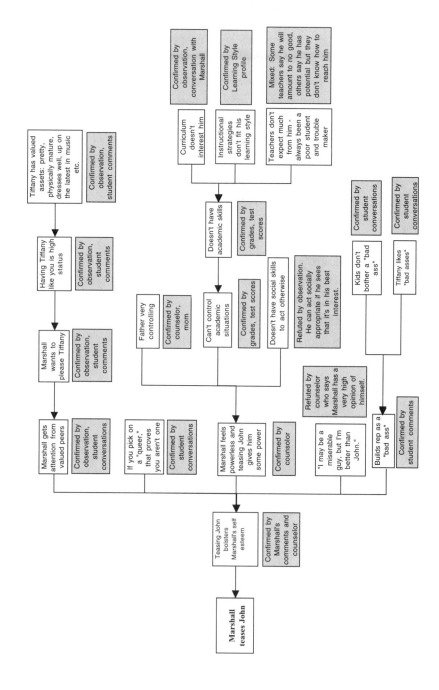

they need to look beyond the situation with Marshall and John, but she also felt strongly that the team might have to come up with a plan tailored specifically to the needs of these two boys.

Mellie started her computer and opened Microsoft® Excel. Drawing from her conversations with the two boys, other students, and Cory's reports, she began building a cause map of the fight between Marshall and John. After an hour's work she had a fairly extensive map. She printed it out and pasted the pages together to create a large rectangle. She put the map into her book bag to share with Cory and Joan on Monday. (See Figure II.11 to see a portion of her cause map. You can view her entire map by visiting our site at http://www.pittstate.edu/edsc/ssls/letendre.html.)

September						
						1
2	3	4	5	6	7	8
9	10	11	12	13	14	15
16	17	18	19	20	21	22
23	24	25	26	27	28	29
30						

Challenge Team Example: Planning Period, Monday, September 17

Throughout the day, Cory led his Challenge Team students through Step 2 of *Targeted Problem-Solving*, tackling the problem: "There's too much mean teasing happening in this class."

Recognizing that Cory really wanted their help, the students excitedly brainstormed possible causes. Even Marshall and John contributed. As they brainstormed, Cory wrote each hypothesis on a 3 x 3 white sticky note and stuck it on an easel chart set up at the front of his room.

"Now that we have about 10 hypotheses, we need to start arranging them to show the cause-and-effect relationships," Cory announced, as he pointed to a large paper rectangle taped to the white board. Lively discussion ensued as the students moved the sticky notes around and came to consensus on how they saw the factors that contributed to the teasing.

"Look, Mr. Raines, we did it. We explained the problem," Twyla declared.

Cory smiled and gestured at the board. "Yes, we've made a good start. So now, we need to find evidence that will show us whether or not we've guessed right."

The class then spent about ten minutes listing the information they needed to either confirm or refute their hypotheses. Cory assigned each work group the task of finding evidence for two of the hypotheses and the room buzzed as the groups made their plans.

Throughout the day, each additional group of students added to the map until, by the end of the day, white sticky notes covered the paper. Tomorrow, the students would share their evidence.

As planned, later in the afternoon, the Challenge Team teachers gathered in Mellie's room for a planning session.

"I know we said we would meet in here, but my students have spent the day creating a cause map that covers my board. Why don't we meet in my room instead so we can see what they've done?" Cory suggested. Once they get settled in Cory's room, they examined the students' cause map.

"I'm impressed," Joan said. "They really came up with some good hypotheses."

"It actually went really well," Cory smiled. "My biggest problem was trying to get them to talk one at a time and to slow down enough so I could write their ideas on the sticky notes."

For the rest of their planning time, the teachers generated additional hypotheses and added these to the students' cause map. Mellie shared her own cause map focusing on the fight between Marshall and John and the team found her ideas particularly helpful in posing further hypotheses. They then turned to the Zoom In/Zoom Out questions on the Thinking Through Violence Worksheet to stimulate additional causes:

- Is there any thing about our curriculum that's causing the problem? our instructional strategies? our procedures? our policies? how we organize for learning?
- Is something schoolwide causing the problem? within a particular grade? within a particular classroom?

Figure II.12 shows a portion of the cause map that contains the ideas of both the students and the teachers. To see the full map, please visit our website at http://www.pittstate.edu/edsc/ssls/letendre.html.

Right before the students filed back into the room, the teachers listed the sources of evidence they could tap to determine which of the hypotheses they added actually held water. As they gathered up their materials and headed back to their respective classrooms, the teachers decided to meet again on Wednesday to review their evidence and continue fleshing out the cause map.

Figure II.12 Portion of the Challenge Team's Cause Map

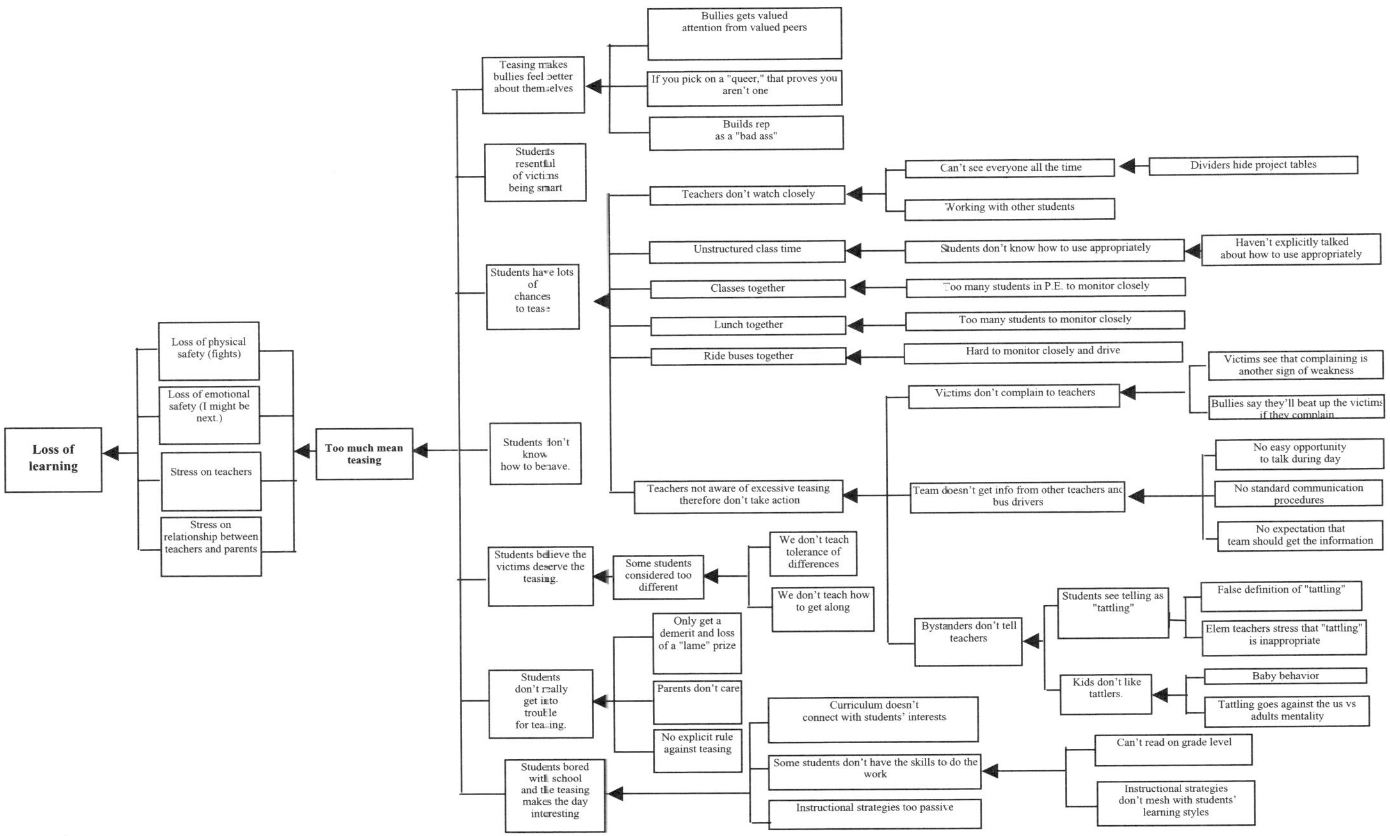

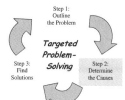

Step 1:
Outline
the Problem

*Targeted
Problem-
Solving*

Step 3:
Find
Solutions

Step 2:
Determine
the Causes

Step 2: Question B— Which Causes Can We Confirm by Evidence?

With Question B: "What causes can we confirm by evidence?" we reach another crucial piece of *Targeted Problem-Solving*. When solving problems, people tend to implicitly generate hypotheses as to why a problem exists. Unfortunately, they simply assume their "pet" hypothesis as true and never even bother gathering any real evidence.

Targeted Problem-Solving, however, requires that you actually gather data and either confirm or refute, *with evidence*, each hypothesized cause you generated. During this fact-finding step, the central question you ask yourself is: "What *objective and credible* evidence do I have to either support or refute this possible cause?"

For example, a policeman investigating a car accident would offer the 80 feet of skid marks as evidence that the car was traveling 65 miles per hour when the driver tried to stop. This represents objective information that others can verify.

Evidence can consist of simple observations, basic measurements, or detailed analyses, depending on the nature of the problem. In most cases, you might already have solid evidence. Often the taking stock information you gathered in answering Step 1, Question C: *How close are we NOW?* can provide evidence. However, in other instances, you might have to gather new data by observing, asking, or reviewing documents.

Of course, you need to check out *all* your hypothesized causes, not just your favorite ones that you feel might prove true. Happily, oftentimes you'll find that one piece of evidence can serve to either support or refute several hypotheses. Thus, your work is really easier than you might suspect.

We also suggest that you strive to obtain at least two pieces of evidence to help you confirm or refute each possible cause. Like prosecutors in a court of law, you should have corroborating evidence. Rarely in a trial does one piece of evidence show, without a doubt, the guilt of a defendant. Rather, the prosecution presents several pieces of evidence that all corroborate and together point to the defendant's guilt. The same logic applies to evidence supporting possible causes. Having several pieces of evidence that all substantiate the same conclusion gives added support to your analysis.

Sometimes, however, you may find that two pieces of evidence point in opposite ways. In such cases, you will have to judge which piece of evidence better represents reality. For example, if your students say on a survey that they watch violent movies and their parents, on a similar survey, say the students don't, you probably would conclude that the students' report is more accurate. Parents may not always know what movies their children see or they don't want to admit that they allow their children to watch such movies.

In other cases, you may find that you need to collect additional data to determine the true nature of the situation. For example, in examining the causes for excessive verbal abuse in your hallways, you generate the following hypothesis: "The excessive verbal abuse occurs in the hallways because adults often don't monitor the hallways outside their classrooms during passing periods."

Teachers indicate on a survey that they do stand outside their classrooms during passing periods, but students say they don't. So what's really happening? In this case, you would want to gather additional data perhaps by unobtrusively observing during several passing periods. Multiple structured observations, as free of bias as humanly possible, can help you understand what's really going on.

Documenting and Summarizing Your Evidence

As you gather evidence and determine which possible causes are actually true, you want to document your findings. First, we suggest that you add a brief statement to your cause map summarizing your evidence for each hypothesis. Second, we recommend color coding your evidence statements, using blue sticky notes for evidence that confirms a hypothesis, yellow for mixed evidence, and pink for evidence that refutes a hypothesis. This way you keep track of what does and does not cause the problem.

Two other ways to visually summarize the results of your evidence-gathering efforts include:

- Force-Field Analysis Chart
- Problem Is/Is Not Chart

Both types of charts allow you to visually document what factors do or do not contribute to the violence problem you face. Not only do these charts identify the causes, but they can also help you determine the strengths that you already have in place. Later in Step 3, these strengths can form the foundation for the solutions you generate. Tool #4 in the Tool Kit explains more about how to construct each of these charts and Figure II.13 shows a Force-Field Analysis Chart that four of Cory's students constructed to document their thinking about the teasing problem.

September						
						1
2	3	4	5	6	7	8
9	10	11	12	13	14	15
16	17	18	19	20	21	22
23	24	25	26	27	28	29
30						

Challenge Team Example: Planning Period, Tuesday, September 18

As Cory came into his classroom after the morning's short faculty meeting, he found his students standing and pointing to the cause map still tacked to the board. "Look, what someone added to our map," Allison said as she pointed to the sticky notes placed on the map by the teachers.

Cory noticed the pronoun—"our"—and smiled. "Mellie was right," he thought. "If we give them a chance, they will rise to the occasion."

Later during class, Cory explained that the teachers used the students' cause map as a springboard for additional hypothesizing about the possible causes for the teasing. The students expressed surprise mixed with pride at hearing that the teachers found their work useful. During the day, the students continued to work in groups gathering the evidence they needed to support or refute their hypotheses. Some of the groups had already found their evidence and shared it with the class. After a lively discussion about the accuracy of their evidence, the students summarized their findings on colored sticky notes, using blue for confirming evidence, pink for disconfirming, and yellow for mixed. As the school day progressed, the cause map took on a blue pattern as the students discovered that their evidence confirmed many of their hypotheses.

September						
						1
2	3	4	5	6	7	8
9	10	11	12	13	14	15
16	17	18	19	20	21	22
23	24	25	26	27	28	29
30						

Challenge Team Example: Planning Period, Wednesday, September 19

In each of Cory's social studies classes, the students finished sharing their evidence and laying it into the cause map. Cory then asked each work group to create a Force-Field Analysis Chart summarizing the evidence on the cause map. (Figure II.13 shows the chart made by one of the afternoon work groups.) Later in the day, Cory planned to share the students' charts with his colleagues.

Figure II.13   Portion of a Student Group's Force-Field Analysis Chart

Created by Allison, Stan, Amed, and Brittany

CONFIRMED Causes

STRENGTHS
Forces working to eliminate or minimize the problem

Teasing makes bullies feel better about themselves.

Students have lots of chances to tease.

Students believe the victims deserve the teasing.

Don't really get into trouble for teasing.

Students bored with school.

Too much meant easing

Students not resentful of victims being smart.

Students can behave if they see they'll get something out of it.

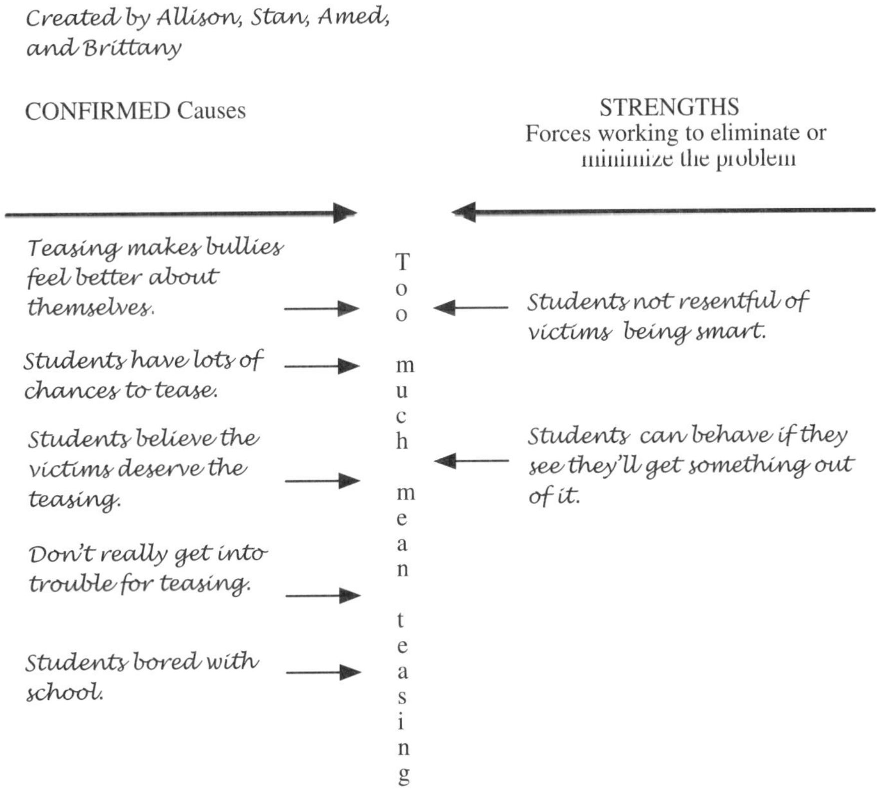

Step 2: Question C—Which Causes Should We Tackle First?

As you review your cause map, you will find that your evidence confirms several causes. Complex problems always have a system of causes and often even simple problems do as well. Of course, you can simultaneously try to address all the causes, but you'll often find that task too difficult. Instead, we suggest that you prioritize your confirmed causes using the following questions and then move only the high priority ones to Step 3. Later, you can cycle back and address your lower priority causes.

Rather than trying to prioritize all your confirmed causes at once, we suggest that you begin by examining only those confirmed causes that directly precede the problem event in your cause map. (See ❶ in Figure II.14.) For the confirmed causes ask:

Figure II.14   Narrowing Down Causes to a Workable Starting Point

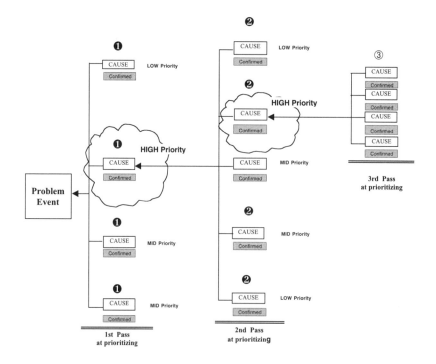

1. If we could remove a particular cause from the situation, would we solve the problem?

2. Which confirmed causes fall within our sphere of influence?

3. Does a particular cause have effects that go beyond the current difficulty?

The matrix in Tool #5 (see Figure II.15) can help summarize your deliberations as you prioritize. The Tool Kit in Part IV includes a full-size blank copy of this matrix. You can photocopy it or download it from our web site at http://www.pittstate.edu/edsc/ssls/letendre.html.

Figure II.15 Tool #5: Which Causes to Move to Step 3

Directions: For each confirmed cause, put a √ in each column where you can answer Yes. After reviewing all causes, assign a priority rating to each.

A: Confirmed Cause	B: If removed, would solve the problem?	C: Within your sphere of influence?	D: Has negative effects beyond current difficulty?	E: Assigned Priority

As you work your way through the questions in Tool #5, you should put a check mark on the form for each "yes" answer. As a general rule, the more check marks for a cause, the higher priority you should give it. We suggest that you use the following guideline in assigning overall priorities to causes:

✓✓✓ = HIGH priority

✓✓ = MID priority

no ✓ or ✓ = LOW priority

If one pass at prioritizing yields a suitable starting point for finding solutions to your problem, you should now move your high-priority cause to Step 3 and begin brainstorming solutions and devising a workable action plan. However, sometimes very complex problems require that you make several successive passes at prioritizing. Figure II.14 illustrates how this narrowing down works. First, you prioritize the confirmed causes directly preceding your problem event. (See ❶ in Figure II.14.) Second, you take the resulting high-priority cause and examine the cluster of causes leading up to that one cause. (See ❷ in Figure II.14.)

Third, using the same three questions listed above, you determine the top-priority cause within that cluster. (See ❸ in Figure II.14.) If you still haven't settled on a suitable top-priority cause to move to Step 3 for solutions, you continue this same process, taking similar successive passes, as you move farther and farther to the right of your cause map until you arrive at a viable cause. In our experience, however, you won't often need to go all the way to the right-hand edge of your cause map. Usually, you can narrow down your confirmed causes to a workable number after just one or two passes.

The key to prioritizing is this: Don't bite off more than you can chew. You should move into Step 3: Find Solutions with bite-size pieces of your problem. Otherwise you may feel overwhelmed, throw up your hands, and revert to old habits, grabbing at the first solution that comes to mind.

After you have devised solutions for your first set of high priority causes, you can cycle back for more "bites" and move your lower priority causes to Step 3 for solutions. Eventually, you'll have a multipronged plan that will successfully address your problem.

An example from an elementary school can demonstrate a first pass at prioritizing. The Responsibility Committee at Clever Elementary School faced a problem during lunchtime: There were too many shouting matches among students. During their deliberations, the group constructed the cause map you see in Figure II.16. They placed the following causes just to the right of their problem event "Shouting matches at lunchtime:"

- Students have little self-control when they get frustrated.

Figure II.16 Shouting Match Cause Map

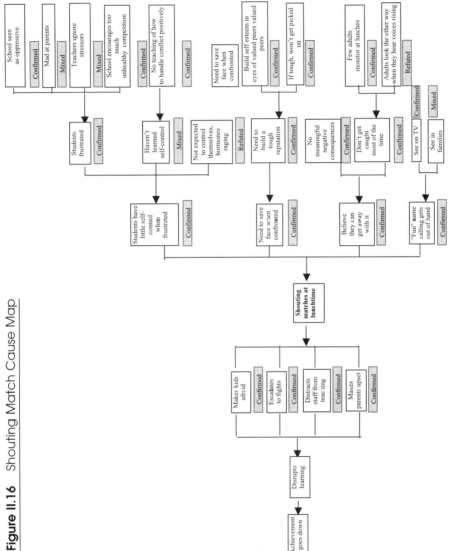

- Students need to save face when confronted.

- Students believe they can get away with it.

- "Fun" name-calling gets out of hand.

Their evidence confirmed all four hypotheses as true. The Responsibility Committee then used the following three questions to prioritize their confirmed causes.

1. *If we could remove a particular cause from the situation, would we solve the problem?*

    A "Yes" answer to this question indicates a prime cause that deserves high priority. As the Responsibility Committee at Clever Elementary completed the matrix in Tool #5 you see below in Figure II.17, they decided that the cause "Students have little self-control when frustrated" rated a check mark in column B of the matrix. They reasoned that if students could develop self-control when frustrated, then students wouldn't engage in shouting matches and the potential for physical fights would dramatically decrease. For the other three confirmed causes, they felt that remedying these would only lessen but not solve the problem.

Figure II.17   Tool #5 for Shouting Matches Problem Which Causes to Move to Step 3

Directions: For each confirmed cause, put a √ in each column where you can answer Yes. After reviewing all causes, assign a priority rating to each.

A: Confirmed Cause	B: If removed, would solve the problem?	C: Within your sphere of influence?	D: Has negative effects beyond current difficulty?	E: Assigned Priority
Students have little self-control when frustrated.	√	√	√	**HIGH**
Students need to save face when confronted.		√	√	**MID**
Students believe they can get away with it.	√	√	√	**HIGH**
"Fun" name-calling gets out of hand.	**Somewhat**			**LOW**

Other prime candidates for a high-priority rating include any cluster where the causes link with the conjunction "and." When all the causes must be present before an effect happens, all you have to do is remove any one of the causes within the cluster and you will prevent the effect.

Building a fire illustrates what we mean by this. To start a fire, you need three things: fuel, heat, *and* oxygen. If any one of these elements is missing, we cannot start a fire.

Figure II.18   The Fire Triangle

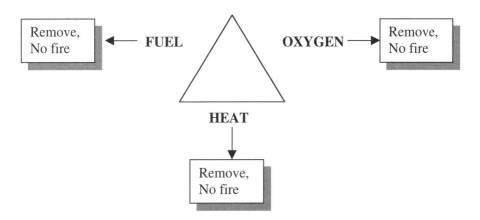

The same holds true with some causes of violence. If we decide that all of the following must be present before a fight breaks out, then all we have to do is to remove one of the causes from the equation and we can prevent the fight:

- At least two students angry with one another, AND

- Students willing to suffer the consequences of fighting, AND

- Opportunity for the students to physically connect, AND

- Students see no alternative other than to engage in a fight.

Unfortunately, most of the causes you will have in your cause map will connect with OR and not with

AND. In that case, you will have to address all the causes within the cluster to prevent the resulting effect. This means you will have to craft a multi-pronged action plan. If, however, you do find a cluster where the causes connect with AND's, then you should give this cluster a high priority and move it to Step 3 for solutions.

2. *Which confirmed causes fall within our sphere of influence?*

Although we educators are a very optimistic lot, often believing that we can work miracles, such is not always the case. Sometimes we simply can't do anything about one of our confirmed causes. If a cause falls outside your sphere of influence (See Figure II.19 below), then you should assign this cause a low priority.

Figure II.19   Sphere of Influence

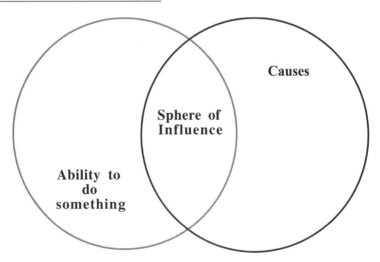

For example, the teachers at the elementary school plagued with too many shouting matches at lunchtime found that one of the causes of the "fun" name-calling resulted from students mimicking what they saw on television. (See Figure II.17.)

Furthermore, evidence indicated that many students saw this same type of verbal abuse frequently in their own families. The teachers felt that they could do little to remedy these two causes. They saw these causes falling outside their sphere of influence. Thus, they assigned the cause "Fun name-calling gets out of hand" a lower priority and resolved to return to it later to see if they could devise any viable solutions beyond having a rule against name-calling.

We suggest that you follow the lead of these elementary school teachers and place low priority causes to the side for the time being, but don't give up totally. You may yet craft a creative solution to a seemingly unsolvable problem, but for now we suggest that you put your efforts toward causes that fall squarely within your sphere of influence.

3. *Does a particular cause have effects that go beyond the current difficulty?*

A cause with broad-reaching effects represents a high priority candidate. For example, the elementary school teachers dealing with shouting matches found that their evidence supported the following hypothesis:

> Students engage in shouting matches because they believe they can get away with it.

The team decided that this "we won't get caught" attitude lay at the root of several other problems in the school, including the recent rash of vandalism. Therefore, the team decided definitely to move this confirmed cause to the Step 3.

As you work to prioritize your confirmed causes in preparation for Step 3: Find Solutions, you may find that your group gets bogged down in its deliberations. Often, simply reminding people that they will later cycle back and find solutions for the lower priority causes will help them agree on which one or two top priority causes the group addresses first.

September						
						1
2	3	4	5	6	7	8
9	10	11	12	13	14	15
16	17	18	19	20	21	22
23	24	25	26	27	28	29
30						

Challenge Team Example: Planning Period, Wednesday, September 19, Continued

At the Challenge Team's planning period, Cory shared the students' Force-Field Analysis charts.

"Cory, you're really getting the kids to do some great thinking," Joan said. "This is really higher-order thinking at its best. I think this teasing problem has become a blessing in disguise for us. We're getting the students to reach new heights. Plus, I do believe we will get this problem solved."

The team then plunged into a discussion about which confirmed causes they should tackle first. They downloaded Tool #5 from the http://www.pittstate.edu/edsc/ssls/letendre.html website and used it to guide their deliberations. Figure II.20 shows a portion of their completed form. They moved four high- and mid-priority causes to the solution-stage in Step 3:

- Students are bored with school.
- Teasing makes bullies feel better about themselves.
- Students have lots of chances.
- Students believe some students deserve the teasing.

For the last 10 minutes of their planning period, the teachers turned to other matters. They planned to do a service-learning unit during November and needed to generate some ideas. They decided to return to the teasing and fighting issue at Friday's meeting.

Figure II.20   Portion of Challenge Team's Completed Tool #5

Confirmed Cause	If removed, would solve the problem?	Within your sphere of influence?	Has negative effects beyond current difficulty?	Assigned Priority
Teasing makes bullies feel better about themselves.	√	somewhat		**MID**
Students have lots of chances to tease.	√	√		**MID**
Students believe the victims deserve the teasing.	√	somewhat		**MID**
Students don't really get into trouble for teasing		√		**LOW**
Students bored with school.	√	√	√	**HIGH**

"But it takes too much time and effort!"

As we've talked about all that you should do in Step 2 to identify causes, we suspect that you a had a voice in the back of your mind asking, "Where can we find time to do all this when we have kids fighting? Things will be in chaos by the time we figure out the causes!"

We aren't suggesting that you do nothing until you identify all the causes. You definitely need to take immediate measures to contain the situation, but if that's all you do, then you have only put a Band-aid on the problem and other fights *will* occur. You have dealt only with the symptom and not the causes and you will find yourself facing the same problems again, and again, and again. We implore you to spend the time and effort it takes to identify the causes and then devise solutions that *really* will be on target.

As for the comment "It takes too much effort!" you're already expending lots of effort dealing with violence problems. In our experience as educators, much of that effort is spent "containing" the situation. We suggest that you change the way you use your effort, shifting from a reactive mode to a more proactive stance.

How much better it would be if we could get in place some *preventive* measures so that the situations in our classrooms and schools don't get to the point that we have "to contain" them? That's what *Targeted Problem-Solving* is all about—finding solutions that address the causes of a problem and then, devising strategies to address these causes. *Targeted Problem-Solving* helps us to "work smarter." Ironically, the better we become at understanding the causes of our current problems, the better we get in being able to prevent them from occurring in the first place.

The Road Ahead

By the end of Step 2, we have identified the causes of our problem. We have a cause map in hand that documents the cause-and-effective relationships underlying the problem. Plus, we have decided which priority causes we want to tackle first. Now, we are ready to move to Step 3 and find solutions. In Chapter 3, we will review this final step in *Targeted Problem-Solving* and continue clarifying each stage with our example from the Challenge Team.

Chapter 3

Step 3:
Find Solutions

"The best way to escape from a problem is to solve it."

Alan Saporta

Introduction

Chapter 3 brings us to the final step in *Targeted Problem-Solving*, the step you've been patiently waiting for. In Step 3, you will use the careful work you did in identifying the causes of your problem and finally craft solutions to reduce the level of violence within your school. We will, once again, use the work of Cory, Joan, Mellie, and their students to clarify our explanation.

Step 3 includes three guiding questions:

1. What are some possible solutions?

2. Which solutions should we implement?

3. Did our solutions work?

Figure II.21   Targeted Problem-Solving

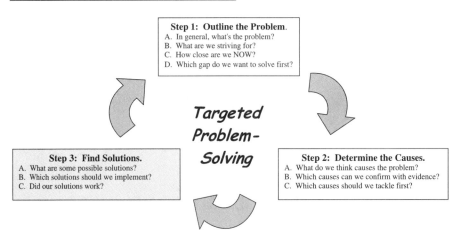

As a reminder, Tool #1, the Thinking Through Violence Worksheet, includes these questions to guide you through Step 3 of *Targeted Problem-Solving*. You can either photocopy the blank form from the Tool Kit or download it from our website at http://www.pittstate.edu/edsc/ssls/letendre.html.

Step 3: Question A—What are Some Possible Solutions?

With Question A, you put your imaginations to work and use the cause map from Step 2 as a springboard for brainstorming possible solutions. Notice that we used the plural "imaginations." That's because we highly recommend that you again involve many voices as you brainstorm solutions. Just as you included people from various groups within your school community in Steps 1 and 2, we also suggest that you ask these same people for their ideas about possible solutions. We particularly urge that you include students. Sometimes "out of the mouths of babes" come the most creative and successful solutions.

At the end of Step 2, you designated one, or perhaps a handful, of causes as high priority. These high-priority causes represent your starting point for brainstorming solutions and, once again, you will find that your cause map can facilitate the process. To focus your efforts, we suggest that you go to your cause map and circle your high-priority cause and its cluster of contributing causes. (See ❶ in Figure II.22.) Then, for each cause, ask this question: "What, in general, would we have to change to remedy this cause?" At this point in the process, you need only list general changes rather than fleshing out exactly how you will make these changes. We suggest that you write these general changes on green sticky notes and add them to your cause map. (See ❷ in Figure II.22.)

Figure II.22 Shouting Match Cause Map with Priority Clusters

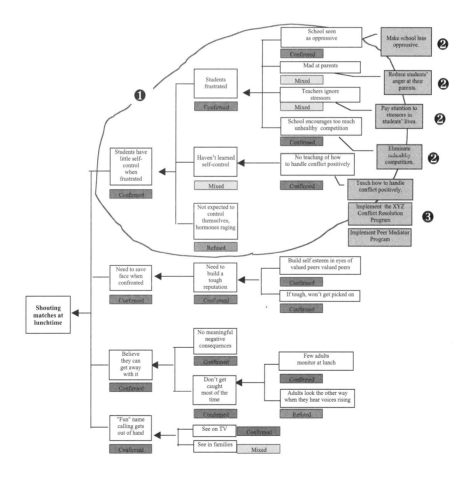

Once you have your list of general changes, you again turn to your cause map, this time as a platform for proposing *specific* ways to make these changes. Working from your cause map, we suggest that you take each cause within your high-priority cause cluster and ask: "How can we change or control this cause?" Notice that we added "control" to our guiding question. Often, solving a problem actually involves controlling one or more of the problem's causes rather than totally eliminating the cause. For example, you may not totally eliminate name-calling among your students, but you can definitely control it and reduce the likelihood of such behaviors occurring at school.

As you brainstorm, we suggest that you list these possible solutions right on your cause map itself, again using green sticky notes. The ❸ in Figure II.22 shows a typical cause-map entry that includes, not only the cause and its supporting evidence, but also possible solutions.

At this point in your search for solutions, you should simply let your creative juices flow. Do, however, try to adhere to the rules of brainstorming and refrain from judging the quality or practicality of the possible solutions. Later, you will scrutinize your list of possible solutions and decide which ones actually have a chance of succeeding. Money, resources, timing, and the impact on other goals will all come into play as you determine which possible solutions to include in your action plan.

As you brainstorm solutions, we suggest that you begin by looking *within* your school for possible solutions. Is there a teacher who appears to have solved a problem similar to the one you now face? Perhaps you can adapt her solution to meet your needs. Is there something you are now doing that you can simply modify? Adapting a solution from within your own school helps increase your chances of success. Such a solution already has shown that it can work within the unique context of your school.

After looking within your own school, you can search beyond for possible solutions. What have other schools done to solve similar violence problems? What do researchers say? A search on the Internet, particularly in the ERIC database (www.askeric.org) will yield several possible solutions. At our website supporting this book (http://www.pittstate.edu/edsc/ssls/letendre.html), we provide annotations for both print and electronic resources that detail what other schools have done and what experts and researchers suggest.

We offer these ideas for possible solutions with trepidation. We know that some people may have trouble resisting the temptation to skip Step 2 of *Targeted Problem-Solving* altogether and go straight to our website and simply grab the first solution that looks good to them. We implore you *not* to short circuit the process. The power in *Targeted Problem-Solving* lies in its ability to match solutions to the specific causes *you* identified in Step 2. Grabbing at the first solution is like grabbing a hammer when you want to cut a piece of wood. You need the right tool for the job, the right solution for the specific cause.

September						
						1
2	3	4	5	6	7	8
9	10	11	12	13	14	15
16	17	18	19	20	21	22
23	24	25	26	27	28	29
30						

Challenge Team Example: Planning Period, Friday, September 21

Cory, Joan, and Mellie left Wednesday's planning session having designated the following confirmed causes as the ones they want to address first:

- Students are bored with school.
- Teasing makes bullies feel better about themselves.
- Students have lots of chances to tease.
- Students believe some students deserve the teasing

Now that they have narrowed down their confirmed causes, they started brainstorming solutions.

Looking at the teasing cause map still taped to Cory's board at the front of the room, the teachers noticed a smattering of green sticky notes that had been added next to several of the confirmed causes.

"Yesterday, the students started brainstorming some solutions," Cory explained. "We didn't get far, but we'll get back to it on Monday."

"It's good that your students are one step ahead of us on this," Joan said. "We can definitely build on what they have done."

The team did indeed pick up where the students left off. Focusing on their four high-priority causes, the teachers made general statements of what they needed to change or control. As they worked, they added green sticky notes that included the following change statements:

Students are bored with school. (HIGH-priority cause)

- Help *all* students acquire necessary academic skills.
- Provide students with a curriculum that interests them.
- Fit instructional strategies to students' learning styles.
- Hold high expectations for *all* students.

Teasing makes bullies feel better about themselves. (MID-priority cause)

- Find ways for students to get attention from valued peers without teasing.
- Help students feel a sense of power and control through positive means.
- Find positive ways to bolster student's self-esteem.

Students have lots of chances to tease. (MID-priority cause)

- Separate teasers and victims during the day (classes, lunch time, passing periods).
- Separate teasers and victims on the bus.

> Beside these particular change statements, Cory placed a note: "Not practical over the long haul. Only addresses a surface cause."

Students believe some students deserve the teasing. (MID-priority cause)

- Convince students that *no one* deserves teasing.
- Explicitly teach tolerance and how to get along.
- Find positive ways to bolster students' self-esteem.

The teachers then went back and started adding specific strategies beside each general change statement. Soon green sticky notes abounded on the cause map.

"We've come up with a lot of good ideas and so have the students," Joan gestured toward the cause map. "But I think we also need to get ideas from other people."

"Like whom?" Mellie queried.

"I'd like to get on the Internet and find out what other schools have done and what experts suggest that we do in dealing with cases like these," replied Joan. "I particularly want to check out the hotlinks on that website where we downloaded this Working Through Violence Worksheet." Joan held up a hard copy of the form.

"I'll ask around for some ideas at the districtwide curriculum meeting I'm going to on Monday afternoon," Cory offered.

"And I'll check out what other teams here in the building are doing," Mellie volunteered. "At our next team meeting on Wednesday we can share our ideas and *finally* start building our action plan."

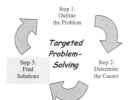

Step 3: Question B— Which Solutions Should We Implement?

Now comes the time to pick the best ideas and design an action plan that addresses the high-priority causes of the violence within your school. In brainstorming solutions, you let your imaginations run unfettered, making no judgments about the quality of the possible solutions. Now, you need to scrutinize each solution and decide which you should implement. The following questions can help you decide which of the possible solutions you might want to include in your action plan.

- *Which solutions will give you the broadest impact, solving several causes at one time?*

  Some solutions can remedy many causes at one time. You should consider including such high-impact solutions in your plan. For example, let's say that you identify all four of the following as confirmed causes of the fighting in your school. Plus you decided these represent the causes that you want to tackle first.

  (1) Students don't know how to resolve conflict in a productive manner.

  (2) Students are angry at the world and the people in it.

    (3) Students don't know how to productively deal with their frustration and anger.

    (4) Students don't see the value of solving conflicts in any other way than by fighting.

Implementing a conflict resolution curriculum that includes an anger-management piece might be a possible solution to all four of these causes.

- *Which solutions can you implement with current resources?*

- *Which solutions represent remedies already in place and would require just a bit of tweaking?*

- *Which solutions have proved effective in school settings similar to yours?*

- *Which solutions meet the requirements of the change equation?*

Earlier in Chapter 1 of this section, we said that people won't change unless they have:

    (1) A shared dissatisfaction with the way things currently stand,

    (2) A sense of do-ability, the belief that they have the resources, skills, time, and energy to make the change, and

    (3) A shared vision of what they're striving for after the change occurs.

Indeed, Figure II.23 shows the full change equation. *All* three of these conditions must exist for successful change to happen. Furthermore, the sum must exceed the costs of changing, such as emotional stress, time, energy, and money. If you have a solution where all pieces of this equation are already in place, you should consider including this solution in your action plan.

Figure II.23   Successful Change Equation

Successful change happens when:

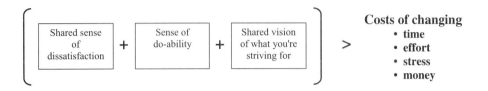

$$\left[\boxed{\begin{array}{c}\text{Shared sense}\\\text{of}\\\text{dissatisfaction}\end{array}} + \boxed{\begin{array}{c}\text{Sense of}\\\text{do-ability}\end{array}} + \boxed{\begin{array}{c}\text{Shared vision}\\\text{of what you're}\\\text{striving for}\end{array}} \right] >$$

Costs of changing
- **time**
- **effort**
- **stress**
- **money**

Creating an Action Plan

At this point, you have decided which solutions you want to implement. Now, you need to put these solutions into an action plan. We suggest that in your action plan you specify *who* will *do what* by *when*. Plus, you should delineate how you will evaluate the effectiveness of your solution. What evidence will you gather to show whether or not your solution actually worked?

We offer the form shown in Figure II.24 as a guide in preparing your action plan. (Tool #6 in The Toolkit provides a full-page version you can duplicate or you can download the form from our website at http://www.pittstate.edu/edsc/ssls/letendre.html.) Notice that this form requires that you specify your confirmed cause along with the supporting evidence. This helps remind you to stay on target and write an action plan that *specifically* addresses the confirmed causes.

We also recommend that you construct an implementation timeline as part of your action plan. We've found through the years that this visual timeline really helps people stay on track when they tackle major tasks. Many have found that creating a wall poster of their timeline serves as a frequent reminder of where they are and what they still need to do. In the Tool Kit and on our website, we provide a blank version of Tool #7: Gantt Timeline Chart that you see in Figure II.25.

Figure II.24   Portion of an Action Plan Form Tool #6

Date: _____   Committee: _____

Confirmed Cause:

Evidence confirming cause:

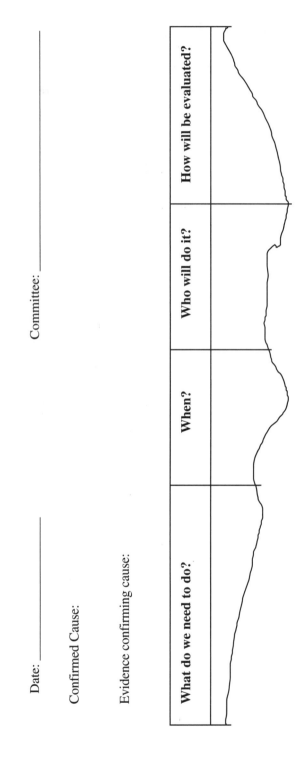

What do we need to do?	When?	Who will do it?	How will be evaluated?

Figure II.25 Illustration of a Completed Tool #7: Gantt Timeline Chart

Place months along here--->	Sept	Oct	Nov	Dec	Jan	Feb	March	April	May	June
TASKS										
Pose evaluation questions	▓									
Establish judgment criteria	▓	▓								
Make plan		▓								
Collect attendance data			▓		▓	▓	▓			
Analyze attendance data								▓	▓	
Conduct student survey (sample)								▓		
Analyze student survey data									▓	

Maintain Unity of Purpose within the System

Throughout this book we've stressed the concept that your school represents a system that includes a variety of subsystems. As you create your action plan, you should keep these subsystems in mind. To successfully implement your solutions and reduce the level of violence within your school, your plan must make sure that all the subsystems within the school work in unison, complementing rather than contradicting one another.

For example, if you decide one of the solutions to the fighting in your school is a change in the discipline code, then all aspects of your school must focus on this effort. Everyone and everything that happens should help to further your effort at reducing the fighting. This means that Ms. Brown's classroom rules on fighting should correspond with the rules her grade-level colleagues use, which in turn should match the schoolwide rules. In other words, the effectiveness of the new no-fighting rules requires that the adults at *all* levels within the school work in unison, with consistency and clarity.

We've seen too many good solutions go down the drain merely because people were working, often unconsciously, at cross-purposes. After all your hard work in identifying the causes of your violence problems and generating solutions to address those problems, don't let poor implementation ruin your solutions.

Do You Pilot Test or Not?

Now, you're ready to implement your action plan. You can, of course, make wholesale changes. However, you might want to simply pilot test your solution before going schoolwide. As you decide whether you should implement a full-blown plan or simply pilot test, weigh the following.

- *How much time, money, and effort will the plan require for success?*

    If your action plan will take a great deal of resources and effort to implement, you should consider conducting a small-scale pilot test before making such a huge commitment.

- *How high are the costs of failure?*

  If the consequences of failing to successfully implement your solution are great, you should think about pilot testing your solution before scaling-up to a full-blown action plan. A pilot test can provide you with invaluable lessons that can help you fine-tune your solution. Also you should contemplate doing a pilot test if your action plan might result in irrevocable negative outcomes. Don't plunge into a solution if you feel you cannot undo your mistakes.

- *How pressing is the problem?*

  If you have the luxury of time because you don't find yourself in a crisis situation that requires an immediate solution, do a pilot test. However, if you find yourself pressed for a solution now, by all means implement your action plan. But DO NOT skip any of the *Targeted Problem-Solving* steps! Especially be sure to hypothesize possible causes of the problem AND gather data that will either confirm or refute your hypotheses. Brainstorm solutions and create an action plan for only those causes that your data confirm. Even when you feel overwhelmed, take time to define the problem. Otherwise, your quick fix will be no fix!

- *Do you have enough agreement among the members of the school community to successfully implement your action plan?*

  Some action plans require that key members of the school community actively support your solution plan. If you don't yet have enough willingness from the key actors, you should consider conducting a pilot test. Many teachers, administrators, students, and parents will take a wait-and-see attitude if your action plan requires major changes on their part. A successful pilot test can go a long way toward convincing people that they should become part of the solution.

September						
						1
2	3	4	5	6	7	8
9	10	11	12	13	14	15
16	17	18	19	20	21	22
23	24	25	26	27	28	29
30						

Challenge Team Example: Planning Period, Wednesday, September 26

Throughout the week, students continued to add more possible solutions to the cause map on Cory's board. The teachers have also been busy, individually talking with people, checking the Internet, and brainstorming additional solutions. Today, during their team planning time, they shared their thoughts and began crafting an action plan. Using the following questions to guide their choices, they considered which strategies they wanted to implement:

1. Which solutions will yield the biggest impact, solving several causes at one time?
2. Which solutions can we implement with the current resources?
3. Which solutions represent remedies already in place and would require just a bit of tweaking?
4. Which solutions have worked in school settings similar to ours?
5. Which solutions meet the requirements of the change equation?

The teachers put about half of their possible solutions into a "LATER" file and then sorted the remaining solutions into two categories:

- Can start on these immediately.
- Need some time to implement.

In particular, Joan and Cory decided to adopt some of Mellie's classroom management techniques. Very little of the teasing had occurred in Mellie's classroom and they discovered that Mellie's techniques helped create and maintain a learning atmosphere based on mutual respect. Plus, Joan and Cory recognized that consistency across the team would help boost a sense of unity among themselves and their students.

Cory printed off three blank forms from the http://www.pittstate.edu/edsc/ssls/letendre.html website: Tool #6: Action Plan, Tool #7: Gantt Timeline Chart, and Tool #8: Evaluation Planning Matrix. Blending practicality, common sense, and the potential for effectiveness, the team crafted a plan to solve the teasing problem. (See Figure II.26 for a portion of this plan.) They also recognized that this plan represented a major step toward addressing their broader priority of creating an emotionally *and* physically safe learning environment for all students.

The teachers' excitement increased as they sketched out their action plan. They felt energized and could barely wait until Monday so they could try out some of their new strategies.

As their planning period drew to a close, Cory volunteered to work over the weekend to flesh out the action plan and create a draft implementation timeline using the Gantt Timeline Chart from Tool #7.

"Sunday night, I'll send you an email with the files attached," he promised.

The teachers also agreed that Cory should continue his work with the students, walking them through the last steps in *Targeted Problem-Solving*. Next week, Cory would get the students' reactions to the action plan and have them work together on Gantt Timeline charts for implementing various solutions.

Joan volunteered to draft an evaluation plan to measure the effectiveness of their solutions and the team decided to use next Wednesday's team-planning time to finalize their plans.

Figure II.26 Portion of the Challenge Team's Action Plan

Date: _September 26_   Committee: _Challenge Team_

Confirmed Cause:
- Students are bored with school.
- Teasing makes bullies feel better about themselves.
- Students have lots of chances to bully.
- Students believe some students deserve bullying.

Evidence confirming cause:
Conversations with students, teacher observations, student surveys

What do we need to do?	When?	Who will do it?	How will we evaluate the effectiveness of our efforts?
Institute class meetings and have students devise classroom rules that deal specifically with teasing.	October 1	Joan	Chart incidents of teasing/fighting throughout the year (Students will do in Mellie's math class.)
Implement "We Care" curriculum to teach tolerance and social skills.	October 15 thru May	Mellie and Cory Counselor	Administer pre/post surveys to students and parents concerning teasing, student attitudes toward others, and student opinions about curriculum and instructional strategies.
Create integrated unit centered about the shopping mall.	December	Cory, Mellie, Joan	
Adopt Mellie's classroom management strategies across the team.	October 1	Joan and Cory	Compare content of student journals prior to fight between Marshall and John and afterward.
Rearrange classrooms so can monitor easily.	October 1	Cory, Joan, Mellie	

Step 3: Question C— Did Our Solutions Work?

Once you've implemented your action plan, you need to ask the tough question: "Did our solutions work?" Unfortunately, many problem-solvers never get to this step in *Targeted Problem-Solving.* They believe they have "solved" the problem simply because they implemented the plan. "How could it *not* work?" they say. "We carefully designed our solutions and even more carefully implemented them." But simply *doing something* doesn't always guarantee success. You need to gather evidence to verify the effectiveness of your solutions.

No matter the scope of your intervention, whether it affects the entire school or just a few students, you should always determine whether or not your solutions solved the problem. An evaluation can consist of an year-long endeavor of gathering, analyzing, and interpreting evaluation data or a much less involved effort by one teacher collecting outcome data on her own students.

In a nutshell, the evaluation process follows six steps:

1. Pose your evaluation questions.
2. Establish your judgment criteria.
3. Make your evaluation plan.
4. Gather your data.
5. Analyze your data.
6. Interpret your data.

Appendix A includes a short article, published in the Winter, 2000 issue of the *Journal of Staff Development,* that gives a brief explanation of how to use these six steps to evaluate the effectiveness of your solutions. Also, we have published two other books that give full explanations of these six steps. Like this book, we use extended case studies to show how teams of teachers followed these six steps. Both books, *An Elementary Educator's Guide to Program Evaluation* and *Getting Answers to Your Questions: A Middle School Educator's Guide to Program Evaluation,* provide the same basic information. However, we've tailored the extended examples specifically to the particular grade level targeted by each book. You can visit our website at http://www.pittstate.edu/edsc/ ssls/letendre.html to find more information about these two books, along with annotations and hot links to print and Internet resources that can help you plan and conduct an evaluation of your solutions.

As you plan how you will verify the effectiveness of your solutions, we suggest that you keep the following key points in mind:

- Decide *before* you implement your solution, what kind of evidence will convince you (and others) that your solution succeeded or failed.

- Consider using existing data collection procedures whenever possible, but don't shy away from collecting new data.

  Daily, people within your school collect data that you might use to gauge the effectiveness of your solutions. For example, the principal's office keeps records on disciplinary referrals, absences, and tardies. Also in Step 1, you collected information as you took stock of your vision of a safe school. Perhaps some of these data can serve as a baseline for judging the progress you make in reducing the violence within your school.

- Make a plan on how you will collect this evidence.
  Tool #8 in Part IV provides a matrix that can help you do this. You can either photocopy the form in this book or go to our website at http:// www.pittstate.edu/edsc/ssls/letendre.html and download a copy.

- Collect the evidence.

- Then, *use* the evidence to judge success or failure.

So, What If the Problem Still Persists?

If your evaluation of the solution's effectiveness shows your solution worked and successfully alleviated the problem, then congratulate yourself. If, however, you find that your solutions fell short, you need to step back and ask, "Why did our solutions not work?" Perhaps it has something to do with the implementation of your solutions. Perhaps it has something to do with the match between the causes and the solutions. Or perhaps you missed identifying a key cause in Step 2.

We suggest that you confront this lack of success with the same methodical analysis that you used to arrive at your initial solutions. Indeed, we suggest that you employ the same *Targeted Problem-Solving* steps to now examine why your solutions did not work.

For example, let's say the fighting problem still exists within our school even after we implemented a conflict-resolution curriculum and a new discipline code. How should we proceed?

First, we would outline the problem, asking the four key questions of Step 1 in *Targeted Problem-Solving*:

A. *In general, what is the problem?*

Our solutions aren't working. The fighting still persists.

B. *What are we striving for?*

Here we would consult our action plan and delineate the behaviors and outcomes we expect. For instance, let's say the action plan included a new discipline code. Our outcomes for this piece might consist of:

- All students will know and understand the new discipline code.

- All adults in the school (certified and non-certified) will know and understand the new discipline code.

- All adults in the school will enforce the new discipline code with consistency and fairness.

C. *How close are we NOW?*

In this step, we would gather information that would tell us if indeed these expected outcomes are actually in place. We would use surveys, interviews, observations, and perhaps even review of documents to ascertain if all students and adults know and understand the new discipline code and if all adults enforce the new discipline code with consistency and fairness.

D. *Which gap do we want to solve first?*

If we find that all our expected outcomes are NOT in place, then we now know where we need to begin with Step 2: Identify causes. In Step 2, we would ask: "Why don't the students and adults know and understand the new discipline code?" or "Why don't all the adults enforce the new code with consistency and fairness?"

In some cases, however, we may find that we have no gaps between what we expect and what we currently have. In other words, all the students and adults *do* know and understand the new discipline code and all adults *do* enforce the new discipline code with consistency and fairness, and yet the fighting still persists.

In this circumstance, we still need to move to Step 2: Identify causes, but our question now becomes "Why does the fighting still persist?"

At this point, we move into Step 2 and answer the following three questions within that step:

A. *What do we think causes the problem?*

B. *What causes can we confirm with evidence?*

C. *Which causes do we want to tackle first?*

If our work in Step 1 indicates that the reason our solutions haven't worked is because people really haven't fully implemented our solutions, then our deliberations would center around questions such as:

"Why don't people know and understand the new code?"

"Why don't the adults properly enforce the new code?"

"Why haven't we properly implemented our solutions?"

We would hypothesize all the possible causes of poor implementation, gather evidence to either confirm or refute our hypothesized causes, and put our confirmed causes into a cause map. We would then decide which of the confirmed causes we want to move to the solution stage in Step 3.

If, however, our work in Step 1 shows that we did indeed properly implement our solution, then we need to consider other possibilities as to why our solutions aren't working and the fighting persists. The following questions may help in our deliberations:

- Have we given our solution enough time for the "treatment" to take effect?

- Is our solution for this cause comprehensive enough to address our targeted cause? In other words, do we need to increase the "dosage"? Perhaps we need to refine the discipline code itself or perhaps we need to take extra steps to augment the discipline code.

- Did we fail to move a key confirmed cause to Step 3 when we decided at the end of Step 2 which of the confirmed causes we would move to the solution stage? Perhaps this cause has a greater impact than we thought and now we need to find solutions to address it.

- Did we overlook a key cause of the fighting when we hypothesized possible causes of the fighting in Step 2? Perhaps this unnoticed cause is thwarting our efforts to reduce the fighting.

Once we complete our deliberations in Step 2 and identify the causes why our solutions aren't working, we then move to Step 3 and find solutions to address those causes. As before, the following questions would guide our work in Step 3:

A. What are some possible solutions?

B. Which solutions should we implement?

C. Did our solutions work?

As you have probably guessed by now, with some very complex problems, you may have to recycle through the *Targeted Problem-Solving* steps several times before you have fully solved your problem. Our work with schools has shown that such persistence pays off and schools *do* remedy the complex problems they face. The key is this: Stay faithful to the process. Don't skip steps.

December						
						1
2	3	4	5	6	7	8
9	10	11	12	13	14	15
16	17	18	19	20	21	22
23	24	25	26	27	28	29
30						

Challenge Team Example: Planning Period, Friday, December 7

In late September, the teachers had finalized their action plan and had also drawn up a plan for evaluating the effectiveness of their efforts. (See Figure II.27 below.) By the second week in October, they had their interventions in full swing. Over the next weeks, the teachers saw improvement. Even the students commented on the change in the atmosphere in their classrooms. Things were better but not perfect. The teasing had decreased but had not stopped completely. Occasionally tempers flared, but no further fights had occurred.

At today's meeting, the Challenge Team teachers reviewed the evaluation plan they completed in September. (See Figure II.27.) The team poured over the data they and their students had collected over the past months. They worked to answer the tough final question of *Targeted Problem-Solving: Did it work?*

Mellie shared a graph her students constructed during math class. Starting with the first day of school until yesterday, the students charted the number of incidents of teasing, arguments, and fights that had occurred within the Challenge Team.

Figure II.27   Portion of Challenge Team's Tool #8: Evaluation Planning Matrix

A Evaluation Question	B Information needed?	C Using what method?	D Who will collect?	E By When?	F How analyze?
1. Did the teasing decline/stop?	Number of incidents reported over this school year	Disciplinary referrals Behavior logs kept by teachers	Mellie and students	On-going with report at end of May	Line graphs, examine trend
2. Did we create emotionally/physically safe classrooms?	Students /parents attitudes on classroom climate, teasing, tolerance of differences, curriculum, instructional strategies	Pre/post student survey Pre/post parent survey	Cory, Mellie Students	Pre in October Post in April	Test to see if significant difference between % Oct and April
		Review of student journals	Joan	April	Note patterns before and after fight between Marshall and John

"Looks like we're on the right track," Cory said.

"Yes, I think all we need to do is keep fine-tuning our strategies," Mellie agreed. "My students will continue graphing the incidents and as we get near the end of school, we'll start collecting and analyzing the survey and interview data we need. At the end of the school year, we three can review everything and decide if our solutions have really worked."

Joan walked over to the computer printout on the classroom wall and pointed to the cause map they and the students had created back in September. "I'm particularly glad that we involved the students in handling this. They really came to own this problem and that ownership put us more than half-way toward solving it."

She paused and then continued. " And you know I feel like I've really grown as a professional. I've learned as much as the students have from tackling this problem. This is why I went into teaching!"

Mellie and Cory nodded in agreement.

	June					
						1
2	3	4	5	6	7	8
9	10	11	12	13	14	15
16	17	18	19	20	21	22
23	24	25	26	27	28	29
30						

Last Day!

Challenge Team Example: Planning Period, Day after School Dismissed for Year

Cory, Mellie, and Joan sat around the conference table in Mellie's classroom. Books, papers, and files covered the surrounding student desks.

"Before I put all this away for the summer break, I want to show you the data the students collected and analyzed." Mellie said as she passed out copies of a five-page typed report, with several tables and line graphs included.

"The students finalized this last week," she explained. "Cory, on page two you'll find the table summarizing the information the students collected using the surveys they created in your class. It's all positive. The students, their families, and the specials teachers (P.E., music, art, technology, and foreign language) all say we've dramatically decreased the teasing. Furthermore, they see improvement in the students' attitude toward school in general."

The team spent the next 30 minutes reviewing the report. They also discussed how far they had progressed in creating an emotionally safe learning environment within their classrooms. They decided they would continue meeting over the summer to plan for next year.

"You know, last September after such a rocky beginning to the school year, I really didn't know if I wanted to stay in this job," Cory confessed, "but the year turned out great! I feel energized even though I'm exhausted and need a break. I'm even looking forward to next year."

Joan and Mellie smiled in agreement. It *had* been a good year and next year would be even better!

An Alternative View

As you read through our extended example showing how the Challenge Team teachers addressed the fighting and teasing among their students, you may have found yourself viewing their problem differently. Furthermore, you may have even thought of some viable solutions that the Challenge Team teachers did not see. Rather than declare Cory, Mellie, and Joan "wrong," we want to stress that complex problems often have many different pathways to solution. Indeed, the power of *Targeted Problem-Solving* lies in its capacity to incorporate many viewpoints and yet mesh these diverse ideas into a viable action plan tailored to the specific situation within a school or classroom. The fact that you do see alternatives beyond those voiced by Cory, Joan, and Mellie underscores our recommendation that you seek the help of others as you grapple with the violence issues you face in your classroom or school. Yes, it is possible to "fly solo" with *Targeted Problem-Solving*. However, we have always found that problem solving with others, even one other person, significantly broadens our perspectives and expands the likelihood that we will craft a successful solution.

The Road Ahead

In Part II, we devoted a chapter to each of the three steps in *Targeted Problem-Solving*, showing you through explanation and example how to find solutions that will effectively address the violence you face in your school. The next part of the book provides another extended example. This time we show how an entire school used the process to address vicious rumor mongering and bullying among its female students.

Part III

An Epidemic of "Queen Bee" Bullies[42] at Smartberg High School

Introduction

Monday, during 1st period

"Ms. Noland, please let me go home," Carrie begged between sobs. "I just can't go to class today. They're in almost all of my classes! They're after me. Everyday they're after me," Carrie said as she blew her nose. "Just look at this. I found it taped to my locker this morning," Carrie handed the counselor a wadded up piece of paper.

The counselor unfolded the paper to reveal the word "SKANK" written above a crude, sexually explicit drawing.

Cheryl Noland listened as Carrie sobbed, "And everyone knows. They stare at me in the halls, at lunch, even in class. Everyone believes what they're saying about me!"

Carrie continued to catalog the sexual remarks, the mysterious notes, the rumors, and even the threats she had received over the past week at the hands of Shana Welts and her clique of three sophomore girls.

Thirty minutes later Carrie left Cheryl Noland's office still upset and still unwilling to return to class. Cheryl wrote the ninth grader a pass to the library for the remainder of the class period.

"Do you have time to talk?" she asked Henry Chen as she poked her head into the assistant principal's office.

"Sure," Henry replied as he motioned her in. "Besides I've been meaning to talk with you."

"Henry, Carrie Moellner just left my office. I wrote her a pass to the library until third period," Cheryl explained. "She came in crying, refusing to go to class. She says that some tenth grade girls are after her. This is the fifth freshman girl this week that has come in with the same complaint. I think we have an epidemic of girl bullies on our hands!"

"That's exactly what I wanted to talk with you about," Henry said. "I spent the better part of yesterday trying to get to the bottom of who's been sending some pornographic mass emails about a freshman girl. Her mother was livid and the girl was a basketcase. The mom printed one out for me to see and I tell you it's sick!"

"I think we need to do something about this now," Cheryl stressed. "I think we're seeing only the tip of the iceberg. This *will* escalate!"

"I'll ask Lydia to put it on the agenda for this week's Council meeting," Henry offered. "But in the meantime, you and I need to put our heads together and see what we can do to help Carrie and the others get through this."

Wednesday, 3:15 p.m., That Same Week

"Looks like everyone's here. Let's get started," Principal Lydia Jones said as she opened the weekly meeting of the Principal's Council. The council included three teachers, all elected by their peers; assistant principal Henry Chen; counselor Cheryl Noland; a representative from the noncertified staff; and, of course, Lydia, the principal.

"We've got three items on our agenda today: the Homecoming Dance, a progress report on our preparations for the upcoming state accreditation visit, and some difficulties among the freshman and sophomore girls. Let's start with the last item first," suggested Principal Jones.

Henry, with Cheryl's help, chronicled the events of the past week involving ninth and tenth grade girls. They described the harassment, the pornographic emails, the notes on lockers, the threatening phone calls, the sexually explicit rumors running rampant among the ninth graders about certain girls, and even the existence of the "Hate Carrie, the _unt Club" whose members signed a pledge to make Carrie Moellner's life hell.

"We've suspended the ringleaders and their minions and gotten some help for the victims," explained Henry. "But this problem is not going to just fade away. The suspensions will put a damper on it for a while, but it *will* rear its ugly head again if we don't deal with the underlying causes."

Heads nodded around the table as Henry spoke.

"We need to get on this right now," Principal Jones said emphatically. "Suggestions?"

"We could put together a group to think this through and bring back some ideas to our next meeting," suggested José Rodriquez, a social studies teacher.

"I agree," said Marsha Collins, math department chair and debate sponsor. "But I don't think anyone can put together a good plan in just one week. This problem is just too complex."

"I see your point," said José, "but I feel we need to get this group going now, if not sooner."

"Henry, would you and Cheryl take the lead on this?" the principal asked.

"Sure," Henry replied after getting the nod from Cheryl. "We'll try to get a meeting together tomorrow afternoon. At next week's council meeting, we'll give you an update."

"Good. We'll put you on the agenda each week so that you can keep us informed," Principal Jones remarked. "We need to deal with this now. It's already gotten out of hand as far as I'm concerned. By the way, you two might look at a book I have in my office. I picked it up just yesterday and the whole book is about this very kind of problem. I think the title is *Queen Bees and Wannabes*.[43]"

Step 1: Outline the Problem.
        A. In general, what is the problem?

1st Meeting of the Task Force, Thursday, 3:15 p.m.

"I'm glad you all could make this meeting on such short notice," said Assistant Principal Henry Chen as he glanced at the 11 people seated around the table. In just one day, Henry and Counselor Cheryl Nolan have recruited the following people to serve on the Caring In: Bullying Out (CIBO) Task Force:

Students:	Nicole, eleventh grader and member of the debate team and captain of the softball team
	Lindsey, tenth grader and member of the Student Council
Teachers:	Kathie Warner, science teacher and cheerleader sponsor
	Scott Rhiner, band director
Parent:	Sandra Ryan, mother of ninth grader Shanice, and twelfth grader Jake. (Shanice has been the victim of some of the nasty rumors.)
Support staff:	Yolanda Sanchez, nurse
	Marla Williams, food-service manager

Community representatives:

Ellie Fernandez, "Y" Program Director

Rev. Harold Williams, youth minister

Betty Logan, child psychologist

"Yesterday, at the Principal's Council, Cheryl Nolan and I raised a concern about what we're seeing among our freshman and sophomore girls. It appears to us that we've got a bunch of girl bullies making life miserable for some freshman girls," Henry explained.

"Yeah, you're so right," Sandra Ryan interjected. "My daughter Shanice has been getting some really nasty phone calls and I want it stopped."

"That's exactly why we've asked you here today, Ms. Ryan," Henry continued. "We need your help in getting all this bullying stopped once and for all. Indeed, we're asking all of you to help us come up with a plan that not only addresses the immediate problems, but also gets at the underlying causes of this vicious harassment."

"Well, you can count me in," Ms. Ryan said. "We've got to do something. My daughter's getting ulcers over this!"

"Let's get started then," Henry said as he handed out an agenda and some yellow sheets titled *Tool #1: Thinking Through Violence Worksheet*. "I would like to keep our meetings to only one hour. Scott, would you act as timekeeper today and let us know when we get down to our last 15 minutes?"

"Glad to," Scott replied as he checked his watch against the clock on the wall.

"To help stay focused, Cheryl and I would like to use the process you see on these yellow sheets," Henry explained.

Cheryl then briefly walked through the three steps and the guiding questions of *Targeted Problem-Solving*.

"The first step asks us to outline the problem," Cheryl explained. "So, in general, what's the problem?"

"Well, that's easy," said Nicole, the eleventh grade student. "We've got some girl bullies making life miserable for some freshman girls."

"Right," Cheryl said as she wrote Nicole's statement on the easel pad.

Girls bullying 9ᵗʰ grade girls

"Now, let's get down some details about this bullying," Henry said as he pointed to the four empty blocks labeled Who, What, Where, and When on the yellow worksheet.

The group outlined the problem as Cheryl recorded the information. Within 20 minutes, they had produced the document shown in Figure III.1.

Figure III.1   Smartberg's Step 1: Outline of the Problem

Who
(Perpetrator? Victims? By-standers? Any patterns?)

* All victims freshman girls -- 16 students reported multiple incidents
* All bullies sophomore girls -- 6 identified
* All members of the bullies' entourage are 9th or 10th grade girls - about 35
* Boyfriends of the bullies and their minions:
  - go along
  - laugh
  - at times help
  - don't think up the ideas
  - enjoy watching the girls "do their thang."
* Victim's friends never <u>publicly</u> stand up for the victim
* Bystanders laugh, rubber neck during the humiliation incidents
* Many 9th graders (boys and girls) talk about the humiliation incidents
  "Can you believe what they did to XXXX today?!"
  "I wonder what they'll do to her tomorrow?"
* No one, except the victims, reports incidents to adults.
* Students reluctantly state what they saw or heard if an adult <u>specifically</u> presses them about a <u>specific</u> incident.
* Junior and senior girls view this as "childish" behavior, part of freshman initiation

What
(*Behaviors* of perpetrators, victims, by-standers, adults. Any patterns?)

* Notes taped to lockers
* Posters on lockers for all to see
* Bully's minions walk down hallway and turn and stare in unison at victim
* Telephone calls -- Threats and name-calling by mysterious callers
* Emails to victim
* Mass emails about victim to students
* Chat room and instant messaging -- sexual remarks about victims
* Pornographic photos - computer generated with victim's face superimposed

"Looks to me that we've definitely defined this problem," commented Henry as he surveyed the sheets on the wall. "Looks pretty thorough to me."

"Wait, I don't think we've finished this section yet," Yolanda, the nurse observed. "The yellow worksheet shows that we need to also examine the impact this problem has on our school's overall goals."

"Right," Henry agreed. "We need to fill in the grid you see on page 1 of your yellow packet."

"Hold on," interrupted Scott. "We all know this girl bullying affects what we're trying to do here. Why do we have to spend

Figure III.1   Smartberg's Step 1: Outline of the Problem (*Continued*)

Where
(*Physical* location of the incidents. Patterns?)

* in the cafeteria, particularly "C" lunch period
* in certain classrooms, where all the "sting triangle" have class together

> NOTE: doesn't occur in Pam Langer's classroom (Computing 101) even though the full "sting triangle" in the same class

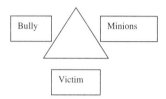

* girls' bathroom near Room 115, freshman wing
* hallways, during change of classes
* parking lot
* victim's locker area
* over the Internet through email/Instant messaging
* First home game -- Boys' Basketball
* Retro Club [popular dance club for 17 year olds and under]

When
(*Timing* of the incidents. Any patterns? Frequency)

- August, September, October - "freshman initiation"
- During unstructured times such as passing periods, lunch, before/after school
- Before school - notes on lockers that victims see first thing in the a.m.
- After school -- first 15 minutes after dismissal
- During "C" lunch period -- mostly 9th and 10th graders at lunch
- First/last 5 minutes of class time in a class where the "sting triangle" have class together
- First home game of the boys' basketball season
- Occurs daily

precious time stating the obvious? We have only 20 minutes left in our meeting."

"I know it seems obvious, but I also know from experience it does help to make everything explicit, particularly if we have to go to the school board and ask for some extra money and resources to solve this problem," Cheryl stated. "The board members are bottom-line folks. They'll want to know how giving us extra money will affect our school's goals, especially student achievement. We'll need to have some answers ready for them."

"Well, I hadn't thought about that," Scott replied. After a moment's pause, he added, "I would say that the bullying is definitely bringing down the grades of everyone in the 'sting triangle,' the victims, the perpetrators, and the bystanders."

The group continued their discussion, reviewing the impact bullying has on the school's overall goals. As they talked, Cheryl completed the grid on the Tool #1 worksheet.

Figure III.2   Smartberg's Impact on School's Overall Goals Outline

Academic Achievement	Grades of victims and perpetrators poor, state test scores low.
Physical safety	9th and 10th graders say they are afraid.
Emotional safety	9th and 10th graders say they are afraid they will be next.
Staff	Frustrated that have to take time away from instruction.
Parents/Community	Parents of both victims and perpetrators frustrated with school, SHS getting a bad reputation within the community.
Accreditation	If test scores continue to go down, school may go on the state's "watch" list.
Funding	A bad reputation may cause voters to not approve upcoming bond issue.
Facilities/Maintenance	No impact yet but potential for graffiti.

Step 1: Outline the Problem.
B. What outcomes are we striving for?

"The next guiding question for Step 1 asks that we define what we are striving for," assistant principal Chen read from the yellow Tool #1 worksheet.

"Well, we don't have to think too hard on that one," Rev. Williams interjected. "We want the vicious rumor mongering to stop. We want the bullying to stop."

"I agree, but I think we also want more," Kathie Warner, science teacher and cheerleader sponsor commented. "We want an emotionally safe learning environment for all of our students."

"That sounds fine with me," replied Rev. Williams, "But just what does 'an emotional safe learning environment' look like?"

"That's what we need to be thinking about between now and our next meeting," Cheryl said. "We all need to talk to people, especially students and parents, and get their ideas about what we're striving for. We need to list the outcomes we want—the behaviors we want to see students and adults doing when we have this problem licked."

"Why can't we just go to the Internet and get a definition of a safe learning environment from some other school or from some expert?" asked Yolanda Sanchez, Smartberg High's nurse.

"Yes, we should look for some ideas on the Internet," Henry agreed, "but I still think we need to ask people, particularly students, for their ideas. We need to get this problem on everyone's radar and to do that we need to start involving everyone from the beginning."

"You're right," Cheryl concurred. "Asking people for their ideas is a good start in getting everybody committed to solving this problem. We can come up with a brilliant solution plan, but if we don't have buy-in from the students, faculty, staff, and parents, our solutions just won't happen."

"OK, I'm convinced," Yolanda stated. "So what should each of us do between now and our next meeting?"

The group used the last five minutes of the meeting deciding how they would get input from students and adults. They decided that Nicole and the rest of the debate team would visit half of the homerooms and ask students: "What would an emotionally safe learning environment look like to you?" The teachers and staff members volunteered to talk with their colleagues, plus parent Sandra Ryan said she would raise the question at the upcoming PTA and Booster Club meetings. Ellie Fernandez, Director of the "Y," and Rev. Williams agreed to gather ideas from their networks of youth workers. Finally, psychologist Betty Logan and Yolanda offered to check out what's on the Internet. Betty especially wanted to look at the website for the Ophelia Project[44], an organization that focuses on empowering adolescent girls.

2nd Meeting of the Caring In: Bullying Out (CIBO) Task Force

"It's 3:15. Let's get started," Assistant Principal Henry Chen said as he looked around the room and noted that all members of the task force had arrived. "Who would like to act as recorder today?" Ellie, from the "Y" volunteered. "And who will watch the clock for us?"

"I'll do that," said Marla Williams, the food-service manager.

"Thanks. We've got lots to do today," Henry said as he handed out the meeting's agenda. "We need to decide what we're striving for—what we mean by 'an emotionally safe learning environment.' And we need to take stock of just how close we are to this vision."

He paused as people read through the agenda.

"Let's begin by just listing some ideas for our vision," Henry directed. "We don't actually have to write out a vision statement. We just need to decide on the general components of our vision. Essentially, we need to list the outcomes we hope to achieve. Nicole, what did the students have to say?"

"The students had lots of ideas," Nicole began. "To them an emotionally safe environment means no bullying at any time, anywhere, by anyone, period. That means no students bullying students," she paused and then continued, "and that means no adults bullying students."

The adults around the table stared at Nicole as she spoke these last words.

"What do you mean 'no adults bullying students?'" teacher Kathie Warner asked incredulously.

"I mean teachers who publicly humiliate students in class, who put down kids, who use sarcasm," Nicole calmly answered.

"This happens a lot?" Kathie asked, still skeptical.

"Yes. The students we talked with say it does," Nicole reported.

"I can't believe such things happen," Kathie countered. "Teachers don't bully students. I think the students are just trying to deflect the blame for all this bullying from themselves to the adults. That's typical. Just blame someone else!"

"I know that this strikes a nerve," Cheryl Nolan, counselor, said. "I don't like hearing it either. However, we need to define what we mean by an emotionally safe learning environment and I think we should include 'no bullying' as part of our vision. What do the rest of you think?"

Heads nodded in agreement around the table, even Kathie's.

Ellie wrote NO *bullying* on the easel pad.

"What other things do we want to include in our vision? What will things look like when the problem no longer exists?" Henry asked.

"Well, students would not to engage in malicious gossip," Marla Williams offered.

"And they wouldn't see it as not 'cool' to bully others," psychologist Betty Logan added.

"Right," Henry agreed, as Ellie charted comments on the easel pad. "Any other behaviors we want to specify?"

Everyone chimed in and Ellie could barely write fast enough.

"So far, all the behaviors say 'Students will,'" noted Cheryl. "What will we as adults do?"

"I think we adults here at the school must take a zero-tolerance stance toward bullying," Scott said. "That means we have to watch for it and take action when it happens."

"And the adults at home and in the community need to support the school's efforts to stop the bullying," Sandra Ryan added.

"That also means that parents should not make excuses for their children when their kids bully others," Rev. Williams suggested. "They should support the school even when their children do wrong."

"In fact, parents should actively discourage their children from bullying others," Marla proposed.

For the next few minutes, the group continued adding more outcomes to the list.

"Does this reflect what we want?" Henry asked as he point to the easel pad.

Everyone signaled agreement.

Figure III.3   Smartberg's List of Outcomes

B. What outcomes are we striving for?

Student behavior outcomes?	*Students will:* · *Not bully others.* · *Not engage in malicious gossip.* · *See it as not "cool" to bully.* · *Not engage in name-calling.* · *Use email and instant messaging responsibly* · *See teachers as allies in combating bullying*
Teacher/staff behavior outcomes?	*Teachers/staff will:* · *Not bully others.* · *Watch for bullying and take action when it happens* · *Create a caring, respectful classroom environment where it is not "cool" to bully* · *Establish trusting, caring relationships with students*
Parent/Family/ Community behavior outcomes?	*Families and youth workers will discourage children from bullying* *Youth workers will create a caring, respectful environment where it* *Is not "cool" to bully*

Step 1: Outline the Problem.
C. How close are we NOW?

Continuation of the Caring In: Bullying Out Task Force's 2nd meeting

"Now, where do we go from here?" Scott asked, looking at his copy of the *Thinking through Violence Worksheet*. "What do we need to do next?"

"Looks like we need to take stock of just how close we are to this vision," answered Ellie as she drew a grid beside each piece of the group's vision. Meanwhile, Cheryl worked at her laptop computer transferring the outcomes to a blank Tool #2: Taking Stock Grid she had downloaded off the Internet.

"It says here that when we take stock we need to rely on evidence and not just our gut feelings," Kathie Warner, the science teacher, said. "This means that we need data, not just speculation or conjecture."

"Well, I would say right off the top of my head that we're far from achieving any of these outcomes," Scott Rhiner, band director, stated.

"I don't know if that's true," Lindsey, the tenth grader said quietly. Everyone looked at Lindsey. She hadn't said much during the group's previous meeting and they wanted to hear what she had to say.

"I think that it's only a handful of kids who are causing all this. Really, most kids don't like the bullying, but they're scared to say anything," Lindsey explained. "If they do, they'll pay for it and be the next target. They're just not willing to take that chance."

"Both of you make good points," Cheryl said. "However, we need some evidence. I suggest that we split up our group and spend the next two weeks gathering information that will help us judge just where we stand on our vision."

"Right," Kathie agreed. "We might need to do some observations, maybe some surveys. We might already have some existing data that we can use."

Following Cheryl's suggestion, the group divided up the taking stock tasks. They assigned one subgroup to gather evidence about the student outcomes, another about the parent outcomes, and still another about the teacher and staff outcomes. To give everyone time to gather evidence, they scheduled their next meeting for two weeks later. They agreed that each subgroup would give a short report at that time.

During the two weeks after the 2nd meeting

During the following two weeks, the subgroup investigating the student outcomes conducted a quick, informal survey of students in randomly selected homerooms. A cross-section of 516[45] students in all grade levels anonymously answered a survey devised by the Task Force members. (See Figure III.4.) Also, the teachers in the school completed a similar survey that asked them about the behaviors of their students and fellow teachers. The teacher survey also asked teachers about the level of cooperation they had received from parents.

Figure III.4   Taking Stock Student Survey

The Caring In: Bullying Out (CIBO) Task Force is working to make Smartberg High School a safer school.
We want your opinion on how things stand around here right now.
Please do not put your name on this sheet of paper.
Your answers will remain confidential.

(1) What is your grade level? (circle one) 9th 10th 11th 12th

Please put a check mark in the column
that best describes your answer.

How many STUDENTS in your grade level do the following?	Almost all	Many	A few	Almost none
(2) Feel it's OK to bully someone?				
(3) Would tell a teacher or administrator if they saw someone bullying another person?				

How often do you see STUDENTS in your grade level do the following?	Many times every day	A few times every day	A few times a week	A few times a month	Hardly ever
(4) Tell mean rumors about other students?					
(5) Call other students names?					
(6) Use emails or instant messaging to say nasty things about another student?					

How many of your TEACHERS do the following?	Almost all	Many	A few	Almost none
(7) Don t allow name-calling or put downs in their classrooms?				
(8) Know when students are being mean to other students?				
(9) Punish students who say or do mean things to other students?				
(10) Have what you consider to be a caring, respectful classroom environment?				

(11) Comments?

Thank you for giving us your opinions.

Others on the CIBO Task Force reviewed the disciplinary referrals over the past school year, looking for patterns. Henry Chen
interviewed his colleagues during the Principal's Council meeting, asking them to comment on the school's status on the task
force's vision for an emotionally safe learning environment. Cheryl
Nolan examined the results from the Healthy Kids Survey[46] that
last year's ninth and eleventh graders completed. She looked particularly at the section that asked questions about bullying and
school violence.

Teachers Kathie Warner and Scott Rhiner and students Nicole
and Lindsey conducted informal observations in the hallways
before and after school and during passing periods, during lunch
periods, and out in the parking lot before and after school. Kathie
and Nicole noted all the positive things that happened in terms
of student interactions, while Scott and Lindsey kept track of the
negative interactions among students. Scott, the band director,
even scripted a name-calling incident that ended with him taking two students to the principal's office.

Finally, at the regular meeting of the Booster Club, Sandra
Ryan got about 55 parents to complete a survey that asked questions similar to those on the student survey. (See Figure III.4.)
Parents also answered questions about what they do at home to
discourage bullying, name calling, and rumor mongering.

Third Meeting of the Caring In: Bullying Out (CIBO) Task Force

"I want to begin by thanking you for all your hard work over the
past two weeks," said Cheryl Nolan, the facilitator for the day's
meeting. "I know it takes a lot of time and effort to take all these
raw data and make sense out of them. Today all this work will
pay off. We'll begin to see just where we stand on our vision for
an emotionally safe learning environment here at SHS."

Cheryl then passed out the meeting agenda.

"Our agenda today includes several tasks," she explained. "First,
we need to share our taking stock reports. Next, we need to complete the Taking Stock Grid that Ellie drew for us last week.

Then, we need to decide which of the gaps we want to solve first. And if we have time, we can start identifying the causes of these gaps."

For the next 30 minutes, each subgroup presented their findings. Kathie handed out a report that summarized the findings from the parent, teacher, and student surveys, including the results from last year's Healthy Kids Survey. (See Figure III.5.) As the group reviewed Kathie's summary, much of the discussion centered on the differences in how students and adults saw things around the school. After much debate, the group decided that the students had a more realistic handle on the situation at SHS.

Figure III.5   Smartberg Taking Stock Report

From Task Force surveys completed last week
Last year's Healthy Kids Survey completed by 9th and 11th graders

STRENGTHS
- As students get older, they begin to see bully as not OK.
- Students in 11th and 12th grades report less bullying, name-calling, and put-downs among their peers.
- Less name-calling among older students.
- Less name-calling than rumor mongering.
- Older students make less use of emails and instant messaging as a forum for rumors and name-calling.
- Fewer older girls report being the targets of nasty rumors, sexual comments, or gestures.
- Few boys at either 9th or 11th grade said that they were targets of nasty rumors, sexual comments, or gestures.
- Boys feel safer at school than girls.
- 11th graders feel safer at school than 9th graders.
- Fewer girls than boys report teasing among "friends."
- More girls than boys feel unsafe at school, with more 9th graders feeling unsafe than 11th graders.
- More girls than boys indicate that they feel badly when someone gets their feelings hurt.
- 50% of the students at both 9th and 11th grades said that they had a teacher or school adult who really cared about them.
- Almost half of the 9th graders reported having a teacher or some other adult at school who always wants them to do their best.
- Over 75% of the students at all grade levels indicate that their teachers will punish those who say or do mean things to others (if they catch them at it), while 100% of the teachers and parents said that they believe that almost all teachers will punish those who say or do mean things to others.

GAPS
- Adults and students differ in their answers to last week's survey. Students say that things are worse off than the adults think. Parents in particular see things in a much more positive light than either the students or teachers. Students indicate that the adults just aren't aware of the extent of the bullying and name-calling that does go on.

Figure III.5 Smartberg Taking Stock Report (*Continued*)

- Over 100% of the 9th and 10th graders said that "Many" or "Almost All" of their classmates think it's OK to bully someone, while only about half of the 11th and 12th graders said that the same thing about their classmates. 60% of the teachers said that "Almost All" students feel it is OK to bully someone.
- Students, particularly 9th and 10th graders, are very reluctant to report bullying when they witness it.
- Students at all grade levels said that most teachers don't know when students are being mean to other students.
- Students say that only about half of their teachers have rules in the classrooms against bullying, name-calling, and put-downs.
- Over 60% of the students said that only a few of their teachers have what they consider to be a caring, respectful classroom environment.
- Students at 9th and 10th grade report seeing daily, frequent acts of bullying, name-calling, and put-downs among their peers.
- Rumor mongering seems to be the more prevalent behavior over name-calling at all grade levels.
- The Internet is just now emerging as a "playground of taunts and bullying."
- Younger students report more use of emails and instant messaging as a forum for rumors and name-calling.
- Teachers and parents aren't aware that students use the Internet as a place to bully.
- Many 9th grade girls report being the targets of nasty rumors, sexual comments, or gestures.
- Teasing among "friends" happens frequently among boys.
- Many girls feel unsafe at school, with more 9th graders feeling unsafe than 11th graders.
- Boys don't seem to be bothered much when someone gets their feelings hurt.
- 50% of the students at both 9th and 11th grades said that they did not have a teacher or school adult who really cares about them.
- 70% of the 11th graders said that there was no school adult who always wants them to do their best.
- Over 1/3 of the students reported having a teacher or some other adult who is mean to them.
- Almost 30% of the 11th grade girls reported having a teacher or some other school adult who is mean to them.

Henry Chen gave highlights of his conversation with the other members of the school's administrative team and Scott Rhiner showed two graphs gleaned from the disciplinary referrals from the past school year and the first months of this school year. One graph charted the number of in-school and out-of-school suspensions each month and the reasons for those suspensions. The other graph showed the number of disciplinary referrals each month over the past 12 months of school, sorted by reasons for referral.

The subgroup that conducted informal observations reported that during lunch, lots of gossiping occurred, but that only about half of the comments fell into the "mean" category. The ninth and tenth graders seemed to gossip the most, particularly before school in the freshmen locker area, in the hallways during passing periods, and after school, while waiting for rides. Girls seemed to start and spread rumors, while the boys simply spread the rumors.

"Let me see if I can summarize what all of you are saying," psychologist Betty Logan said. "It appears that most of the bullying occurs among the ninth and tenth graders and it seems that it's girls bullying girls, not with physical violence but with emotional violence. Am I getting this right?" she asked.

A flurry of "Yesses" answered her question.

"And it seems that the adults here at the school and the parents don't really know the full extent of the rumors, the nasty comments, and the name calling," Betty continued. "Furthermore, most of the younger kids don't see anything wrong with someone bullying another person. Finally, kids feel that some of the adults here at the school bully students."

"I think you've got it in a nutshell," Cheryl commented. "Now that we have heard everyone's information, we need to fill out the Taking Stock Grid that Ellie drew up for us at our last meeting." Cheryl pointed to the large sheets taped to the conference room wall.

During the next 15 minutes, the group completed the grid shown in Figure III.6, with Marla Williams recording the group's decisions.

"Looks like we've got our work cut out for us," observed Nurse Yolanda Sanchez, as she looked at the completed Taking Stock Grid on the wall. "My head's reeling! Things are a lot worse than I ever thought!"

"Things do look pretty bleak," Cheryl agreed, "however, we do have some strengths. Look, they're listed here on the survey results that Kathie handed out. Plus, Nicole and Kathie told us all the good things they saw happening during their observations. Our next task for this meeting is to decide which gap we want to solve first. We have about 15 minutes until our hour's up."

Figure III.6   Completed Taking Stock Matrix

How close are we NOW to achieving our outcomes?							
Column A: Emotional Safe Vision Components	No where near					Fully achieved	Column B: Supporting Evidence??
	0	**1**	**2**	**3**	**4**	**5**	
No bullying	9th and 10th			Teachers not doing enough to stop bullying Students say some teachers bully students	11th 12th Principals suspend when find out about bullying		Task force surveys Healthy Kids survey Observations Principal interviews Disciplinary referrals
Students will: · *Not engage in malicious gossip*		9th and 10th		11th and 12th			Task force surveys Healthy Kids survey Observations Principal interviews

· *See it as not "cool" to bully others*	9th and 10th		11th and 12th				Task force surveys
							   * Student
							   * Teacher

· *Not engage in name-calling*		9th and 10th		11th and 12th			Task force surveys Healthy Kids survey Observations Principal interviews Disciplinary referrals
· *Use email and instant messaging responsibly*	Teachers and parents not aware of students' irresponsible use of Internet	9th and 10th		11th and 12th			Task force surveys Principal interviews Disciplinary referrals
· *See teachers as allies in combating bullying*	9th and 10th		11th and 12th				Task force surveys Principal interviews

Figure III.6   Completed Taking Stock Matrix (*Continued*)

Column A: Emotionally Safe Vision Components	No where near					Fully achieved	Column B: Supporting Evidence??
	0	**1**	**2**	**3**	**4**	**5**	

School adults will: · *Watch for it and take action when it happens*		Students say teachers don't see or know about much of the bullying that goes on			Teachers will punish if catch students bullying others		Task force surveys
							  * Student
							  * Teacher

· *Create a caring, respectful environment*				Teachers not doing enough to stop bullying
				
				Students say some teachers bully students
				
				50% of the students say that they have a caring school adult
							Healthy Kids Surveys Task force surveys
							  * Student
							  * Teacher

· *Establish trusting, caring relationships with students*				50% of the students say that they have a caring school adult			Healthy Kids Surveys Interviews with principals

Families and youth workers will: actively discourage bullying			Parents		Youth workers		Task force surveys
							  * Parent
							  * Teacher
							Interviews with youth workers

Youth workers will create a caring, respectful environment					X		Interviews with youth workers Principal interviews

> ## Step 1: Outline the Problem.
> ### D. Which gap do we want to solve first?

Continuation of 3rd Thursday Meeting of CIBO Task Force

"Seems to me as we look at all these gaps, we should start with something that will give us the biggest bang for our buck," suggested band director Scott Rhiner.

"That makes sense," agreed Sandra Ryan, parent member of the group. "However, we could also start with the easy stuff first, the outcomes that we marked with 3's and 4's. I know that we have to eventually tackle the items we marked with 0's, 1's, and 2's, but I don't think we should bite off more than we can chew."

"Both of you make sense," Cheryl Nolan noted. "I feel it's important that people get a taste of success whenever we start making changes. Plus success will help built up the emotional reserves they'll need for the tough tasks ahead."

"In that case, let's go through our Taking Stock Grid and put an asterisk by those outcomes that would, as Scott says, 'give us the biggest bang for our buck,'" Henry proposed.

Group members signaled their agreement and began working their way through the grid looking first for high impact items.

"Scott, would you please explain more about what you mean about looking for an outcome that will give us 'the biggest bang for our buck.'" Rev. Williams asked.

"Well, I mean we should look for an outcome that if we can get it in place would not only solve our current problem, but would also have positive effects on other things as well," explained Scott. "For example, I believe that if all of us teachers created caring, respectful environments in our classrooms that would solve lots of problems around here, including this queen bee bullying."

"I see what you mean," replied Rev. Williams. "I would like to add another aspect to your 'big bang' definition. I think we should also look for an outcome that, if fully achieved, would make bullying less likely to happen. For example, if students don't see bullying as 'cool' then it is less likely that they will bully others. Right?"

Once again people voiced agreement.

"And if students trusted teachers, they might feel more comfortable telling them about the bullying," interjected Nicole, the eleventh grader.

"Right," Cheryl added. "Plus, trust and caring can have a major influence on how well students learn."

After more discussion, the group finally designated the following outcomes as having the potential for high impact:

- No bullying.

- Students will see it as not "cool" to bully others.

- Students see teachers as allies in combating bullying.

- Teachers create a caring respectful learning environment.

Next, the group highlighted all the outcomes that they had rated as 3's or 4's on their taking stock grid.

"After looking at the overlap of the gaps that we believe will have a high impact and those we judged as 3's or 4's, I think that we should start with the "no bullying" outcome," Kathie Warner suggested.

Everyone agreed.

Kathie continued, "However, I also think we need to go beyond the easy stuff. I don't believe we can actually have zero-tolerance for bullying unless students see it as wrong to bully others and are also willing to tell us when it happens. We can't take action if we don't know about it."

"So you're suggesting that we tackle all four of these gaps at the same time?" asked Yolanda.

"Yes, I think we need to attack this problem on many fronts," Kathie answered.

After about five minutes of further discussion, the task force decided to move all four gaps to the next step in *Targeted Problem-Solving*. They also decided that, out of the four gaps, they wanted to begin by identifying why so many of the ninth and tenth grade girls bully other girls.

"Looks to me like we've completed Step 1," commented Ellie as she finishes summarizing the group's decisions. "Where do we go from here?"

> **Step 2: Determine the Causes.**
>   **A. What do we think causes the problem?**

Continuation of the 3rd Meeting of the CIBO Task Force

"We now start identifying the causes for all this bullying," Cheryl replied. "But I see that we're almost out of time. Between now and our next meeting we all need to be thinking about the possible causes of this bullying," Cheryl explained. "Plus some of us need to talk with people around school and get their input. Nicole, can you and the Debate Team members visit the other half of the homerooms you didn't talk with earlier?"

"Sure, Ms. Nolan," Nicole answered.

"And Lindsey, you're going to talk with the Student Council members at their meeting this week?"

"Yes, Ms. Nolan. I'm always on the agenda to tell them about our work on this committee. This week I'll ask them for their ideas on why girls bully other girls."

Other committee members volunteered to gather ideas from teachers, staff, parents, and community members. Betty once again volunteered to check out what experts had to say on these issues.

"I just had an idea," Ellie interjected. "So that we can be ready for identifying the causes of our other gaps, I suggest that we also ask people why students won't tell teachers when they see someone bullying another student."

"I'm all for working smarter," Scott said. "Let's ask both." Others nodded in consensus.

"Then we all have our tasks. I'll see you next week. This meeting's adjourned," Cheryl announced.

Fourth meeting of the CIBO Task Force

Betty Logan, a local psychologist, arrived at the meeting early. She laid out a handful of marking pens and several pads of 3 inch square sticky notes in an array of colors. Next, she set up an easel with a chart pad. She then taped two long sheets of butcher paper together.

"Can I help?" Sandra Ryan offered as she came into the room.

"Sure, thanks," Betty said. "I'm the facilitator for today's meeting and I want to get everything ready so we can build a cause map of our bully problem. Would you hold up this butcher paper while I pin it to the wall?"

Sandra held one side of the butcher paper while Betty attached it to the wall. The paper covered most of the room's north wall.

"I understand that your daughter has been a victim of the 'queen bee' and her minions," Betty continued.

"You're right there!" Sandra quickly answered. "It's been a nightmare at our house. The suspensions helped, but Shanice, that's my daughter, still doesn't want to come to school. I have to pry her out of bed and force her to get on the bus. She tells me that everyone still stares at her and hardly anyone speaks to her at lunch. She says they all believe what Shana and the others said about her. And I tell you that it was some nasty stuff. They said she had sex with the whole football team, one after another! That's disgusting! I'm at my wits end on how to handle this. That's why I agreed to serve on this committee. I thought I could do something to get all this stopped. No girl should have to endure what my girl is going through," Sandra paused and her voice took on a note of frustration. "But here we are at the fourth meeting and all we've done is talk."

"Yes, we have done a lot of talking," Betty agreed, "but I believe it's valuable talk. We've got to get to the roots of this and that's a hard thing to do. It's complicated and goes beyond what Shana and her clique are doing. I'm glad we're talking about something other than quick fixes, because frankly I don't believe a quick fix exists for this bullying. Even if Shana and her group were kicked out of school, the bullying would still go on."

"You're probably right. I do want to get it all stopped. That's exactly why I joined this group. But I wish it didn't take so long for us to do something," Sandra lamented.

"But if we don't go slow now and carefully examine this problem, our solutions will just go off target and we'll be right back at square one," Betty said. "I believe that the work we've done already will serve us well later when we put together an action plan that really solves this problem."

As Sandra and Betty continued to talk, the rest of the task force took their seats around the table. At 3:15 p.m., Betty started the meeting.

"Today, we move into Step 2 of *Targeted Problem-Solving*; we begin determining the causes of the 'queen bee' bullying we see here at SHS. I want to remind you that our meeting today will last until 4:45 rather than our usual 4:15. We all agreed to stay an extra 30 minutes today so that we can get Step 2 finished. Here's our agenda for our meeting." (See Figure III.7 for the agenda.)

Figure III.7   Agenda for 4th Meeting of CIBO Task Force

Facilitator: **Betty Logan**
Recorder: **Rev. Williams**
Timekeeper: **Danielle**

What	Who	How	Time
1. **Review minutes from last meeting**	Cheryl	Oral report	2 minutes
2. **Generate possible causes**	Everyone	Brainstorm and write on separate sticky notes	20 minutes
3. **Build cause map**	Everyone	Arrange sticky notes on wall	30 minutes
4. **Determine which causes we can confirm with evidence we now have**	Everyone	Review taking stock data	20 minutes
5. **Plan out how to obtain additional needed evidence**	Everyone	Data collection assignments for next week's meeting	15 minutes
6. **Summarize and plan next week's agenda**	Betty	Oral report	3 minutes

After Cheryl read the minutes from last week's meeting, the group drew on their conversations with people around the school and community and started brainstorming possible causes behind girls bullying girls. As they worked, Rev. Williams wrote each hypothesis on a white sticky note and placed it on the easel pad, not worrying about any particular order. He could barely keep up and Marla picked up a marker and more sticky notes and started helping. After just a few minutes, the group generated ten possible causes.

"I think we have enough to start building a cause map," Betty said as she began moving the sticky notes from the easel to the butcher paper on the wall. She arranged them in a vertical line, one under another. She then gave a brief explanation of cause mapping and how it could help the group.

"And once we get this map built, I'll transfer it into an Excel file and send all of you a copy by next week's meeting," Cheryl added.

"Before we go much further I want to add some things to this map," Betty said. "We need to put in the problem event itself." She placed a large purple sticky note labeled *Girls bullying 9th & 10th grade girls* to the left of the line-up of possible causes. (See ❶ in Figure III.8.)

Betty continued. "We'll spend most of our time today backward mapping to determine why girls bully other girls. But I also want us to show what effects this bullying has on our school and it's overall goals. Remember at our first meeting when we were outlining the problem, we listed how the bullying impacts our goals."

The members shuffled through their yellow worksheets to the impact statements they completed as part of Question A in Step 1.

"We need to include this in our cause map to remind us that this problem goes beyond just a handful of girls," Betty continued.

The group then added sticky notes to the cause map to show the effects bullying had on their school as a whole. (See ❷ in Figure III.8.)

Figure III.8   Portion of Smartberg's Cause Map

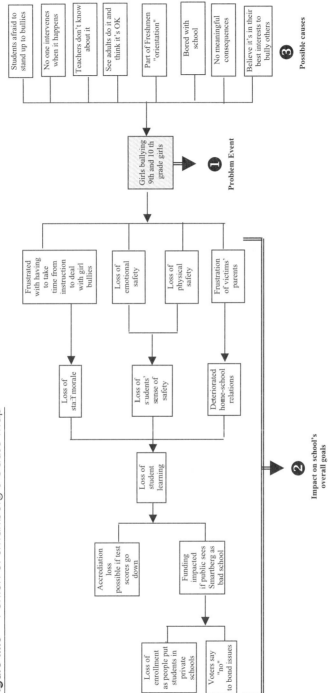

"Now we need to work on fleshing out the right side of this cause map," Betty said. (See ❸ in Figure III.8.)

Ellie, the director of the "Y" spoke first. "I think we need to rearrange some of the causes we've already posted. I really think that when we ask why does no one intervene when the bullying happens, it's because teachers don't know about it and because students are afraid to stand up to bullies. So I would move those two further right as causes of 'No one intervenes.' She pointed to the sticky notes on the wallboard.

People nodded in agreement and Rev. Williams rearranged the notes.

"So why don't teachers know?" Ellie asked, looking at Nicole and Lindsey, the two student members of the task force.

"They don't know because kids won't tell them," Lindsey answered.

"And they won't tell them because kids are afraid that if they tell they'll be the next victims. It'll be payback time for sure," Nicole quickly added.

"And kids don't tell because that would be ratting on someone," Lindsey interjected. "And you just don't do that."

"Why not?" Sandra, Shanice's mom asked.

"Because that's what we've been told since grade school," explained Nicole. "Even our grade school teachers would say 'Don't be a tattletale.'"

"But that's not what your teachers meant," Kathie, the science teacher, asserted. "Your teachers meant that you shouldn't come running to them every time you didn't like what someone did. They didn't mean for you to keep quiet if you saw someone bullying another person."

"Maybe so," Nicole answered, "but I know that a lot of kids wouldn't go to a teacher or principal and tell them what's happening if they saw someone bullying someone else."

"Also, some kids won't tell the teachers because the kids don't see anything wrong with bullying someone," Lindsey said. "In fact, some believe that the victims actually deserve what they get."

"What do you mean 'Get what they deserve'?" Sandra asked. "Shanice doesn't deserve any of this!"

"I agree, Mrs. Ryan," Nicole quickly replied. "But some kids think that people who are really different—you know, dress funny, look funny, act strange, deserve what they get."

"And why can't kids be more tolerant?" asked Mrs. Ryan.

"I think it's because we don't explicitly teach kids to be tolerant of differences," Henry Chen hypothesized. "No where in our curriculum do we teach students how to care, how to get along. We expect that they will just learn how to do this on their own. Unfortunately, it's not happening."

"Rev. Williams, are you getting all this down?" Betty asked.

"Yes, I think so. This is what I have so far," he said as he pointed to the cause map. (See Figure III.9 for the cause map.)

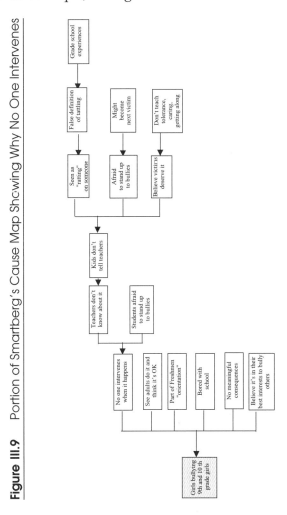

Figure III.9   Portion of Smartberg's Cause Map Showing Why No One Intervenes

"What are some other reasons why teachers don't know about the bullying?" Betty pushed the group to dig deeper.

"Another reason might be because the teachers don't monitor enough," Yolanda, offered.

"And they don't monitor enough because they have just too many students. This is a large school," added Scott, the band director.

"Or teachers don't see it as their responsibility to look for it," Sandra proposed.

The teachers at the table stared at Sandra as she said this.

"You may not like hearing this, but I do think that some teachers here don't see it as their responsibility," Sandra continued. "Most teachers don't say anything in their classroom rules about bullying. Even the school's discipline code doesn't say anything about this kind of bullying. I know. I read through the entire code before I complained to Mr. Chen about what was happening to my Shanice. The code talks about physical threats and fighting, but says nothing about vicious rumors or nasty comments."

"So you're saying that one of the reasons why teachers don't see it as their responsibility to monitor for bullying is because it's not in the school discipline code," Scott asked Sandra.

"Right, that's what I'm saying," she replied. "If it's not important enough to be in the code, then it must not be important enough for teachers to watch for it."

"Rev. Williams, let's add that to our cause map," Betty suggested.

"Now, does anyone else have something they want to add?" she asked.

"Well, we don't have up there one of the most obvious reasons why this bullying occurs," said Kathie Warner. "Students have the opportunity to bully one another while at school because they have so much contact with one another during the school day. The ninth and tenth graders have lockers in the same area, they have the same lunch period and they have several classes together, especially the big classes like P.E., art, and computers."

"Right, let's get that up on the cause map," Betty directed.

"What about that sticky note there," asked Henry, the assistant principal, as he pointed to note labeled *Bored with school*. "Who suggested that?"

"I did, Mr. Chen," Nicole answered. "Lots of kids tell me school's just plain boring. Well, to be truthful, I sometimes get bored myself. And when kids get bored, we do things to make it less boring. I think that's why some kids go along with the bullying. It makes the day more interesting—at least, as long as you're not the victim."

"So why is school so boring?" science teacher Kathie asked.

"Well, Ms. Warner, kids don't like what they have to learn. They don't have any say about what they have to learn. It's whatever's in the textbook or what the teacher wants to do. So much of it seems to have no connection to us."

"You're saying that what we teach here at SHS is useless?" Kathie fired back.

"I'm not saying that what you're teaching is useless, Ms. Warner. I like your class," Nicole replied. "But in many classes it's just the same ol' stuff, over and over since we were in middle school. Plus most of the time in class it's reading from a book or listening to the teacher talk. In some classes, many kids just catch up on their sleep because it's so boring."

"So, tell me again, how does this all relate to bullying?" Rev. Williams inquired.

"Well," Cheryl began. "Bored students breed misbehavior and in this case the misbehavior may result in the kind of bullying we see among girls. During class they gossip, whisper nasty comments, pass notes, and stare at the victim, all because they don't have anything better to do. They aren't engaged in the classroom activities," she explained. "I'm a big believer that if you want kids to behave you need to engage them in something that *they* find interesting. It's a case of competing behaviors. A student can't misbehave if that student is involved in an interesting, meaningful learning activity."

"That makes sense," replied Rev. Williams. "So why don't teachers teach what students find meaningful in ways that engage them?"

That question prompted further additions to the cause map on the wall. The group continued working, taking each of the causes, and digging deeper by asking "Why does this happen"?

They also walked through the Zoom In and Zoom Out questions listed under Step 2 on the *Thinking Through Violence Worksheet*, making sure that they took a systems view of the problem. After a while their cause map filled the wall. (To see the entire cause map devised by the task force, please visit our website at http://www.pittstate.edu/edsc/ssls/letendre.html and click on button labeled "Smartberg Cause Map.")

"This is amazingly complex!" Scott said as he scanned the wall. "How can we ever tackle this thing?"

"It will be difficult. No one said that dealing with a problem like this would be easy, but we can do it," Henry answered. "I remember a quote I read the other day from John Dewey. He said, 'A problem well put is a problem half solved.' I think we're more than half way on this. I'm beginning to see some solutions that will make a difference."

"Hold up, Henry," Cheryl said in a friendly tone. "Let's not get into solutions just yet. We'll do that in Step 3. But let's not forget them either. If some solutions come to mind, jot them down on your yellow sheets somewhere so you can bring them up when we get to Step 3," Cheryl suggested. "We just have to be careful we don't fall in love with our 'pet' solutions. We need to all keep our minds open until we see which of these possible causes actually hold up with evidence."

"You're right," Betty added. "We still need to finish Step 2. We need to see if we have any evidence to support all these causes we've put up on the wall."

> **Step 2: Determine the Causes.**
>   **B. Which causes can we confirm by evidence?**

Continuation of 4th Meeting of the CIBO Task Force

"So what evidence do we have to support or refute all these possible causes?" Marla Williams, the cafeteria manager asked.

"Actually, I think a lot of our taking stock information will help us out here," said Kathie who helped write the report summarizing the survey findings.

"I've found that when I have done this cause mapping in the past, it's easier to begin at the far right and work our way to the left as we judge what our evidence tells us," Betty explained. "This means we start way over here," she said as she pointed to the right side of the map. "For each possible cause we need to ask: 'What evidence do we have to support or refute this cause?' Once we have the evidence, we can determine the true causes."

Betty hands Rev. Williams three pads of sticky notes. "Also, Rev. Williams, let's switch to the colored notes for the evidence. If we decide the evidence confirms our cause, then write it on a blue sticky note, if it's mixed put it on a yellow one, and if it's refuted, then use a pink one. That way we can easily scan our map and see where our true causes lay."

Ellie Fernandez spoke up. "So, beginning on the far right, what evidence do we have to say whether or not students' grade school experiences have contributed to this idea that they shouldn't rat on other students?"

"Well, Nicole says that during the homeroom conversations, the kids told her that's why they won't rat on someone," replied Sandra.

"But that's just one piece of evidence, one view point," Kathie interjected. "We don't know what the elementary school teachers really say, what they're actually doing. We don't have any corroborating evidence on this one."

"Then let's put a question mark by that one until we do get the evidence," said Betty. "How could we get some credible evidence on this?"

"We could ask some of the teachers in our feeder schools. I'd be happy to visit with some of them at our next curriculum meeting," volunteered Kathie.

"Don't you think the teachers will tell you what they think we want to hear?" asked Ellie. "I'm not sure someone would be frank and admit that they aren't doing something they ought to be doing."

"You might be right," Cheryl agreed. "But I would be interested in hearing what they have to say. Kathie, can you come up with some open-end, non-leading questions that you can ask teachers? Perhaps you could ask them how the typical teacher handles this issue rather than how they personally handle it. Then you might get a truer picture. For instance, on our taking stock survey, we asked people to comment on others' actions rather than their own behavior."

"That might work," Betty said. "Also, Cheryl, would you check with your counseling colleagues on the elementary level and see how this 'telling an adult' issue is handled in their curriculum?"

"Sure," Cheryl replied.

"What about our other causes on the right side, any evidence to support one of those?" Betty asked.

"I think we've got plenty of evidence that confirms that students are afraid to stand up to bullies because they believe that they might become the next victim," said Henry Chen. "The Debate Team's conversations in the homerooms verify that. Also some victims tell me that they got targeted just because they defended a victim. In fact, the bullies told them if they didn't go along, they would be next and these bullies made good on the threats."

"Let's put that on a blue sticky note then," Betty said to Rev. Williams.

"That one there. Where's the evidence for that one?" Kathie asked as she pointed to the note with "Adults believe it's part of growing up" written on it.

"I don't think we have any evidence yet to confirm or refute this one. That's another question mark," Betty said.

Lindsey, Scott, and Henry volunteered to gather some evidence by talking with students, teachers, and the principals.

Cheryl spoke again. "Unfortunately, I have some evidence that confirms our hypothesis that we don't explicitly teach tolerance, caring, and getting along in our curriculum at the middle school and high school levels," she explained. "I've reviewed all our curriculum guides and it's nowhere to be found."

"And that goes along with my classroom observations. Teachers don't explicitly teach those skills," Henry added. "With all this pressure for us to improve our scores on the state assessments and the ACT, many teachers aren't taking time out to cover these issues."

"Would this also fit as evidence?" Nicole asked. "Here on our taking stock report it says that over 60% of the students feel that only a few of their teachers have what they consider to be a respectful, caring classroom."

"I'd say that confirms it," said Ellie.

Using the taking stock report handed out during the last meeting, the group continued to work through the cause map, adding evidence and deciding how to gather additional evidence during the coming week. By the end of the 90 minutes, the task force had added the evidence sticky notes, made judgments as to whether the evidence confirmed, refuted, or showed mixed results, and planned how to gather additional information for those causes that had a question mark beside them. They also decided that at next week's meeting they would finalize their cause map, decide which confirmed causes to move to the solution stage, and hopefully start brain storming solutions to remedy these confirmed causes. (See Figure III.10.)

The Next Day Following the 4th Meeting of the CIBO Task Force

True to her word, Cheryl brought her laptop into the conference room the day after the CIBO meeting and transferred the cause map from the wall into an Excel file. As she worked, Henry came in.

"You're not going to take that down when you're finished are you?" he inquired.

"Why, you think we should leave it up?" she asked.

"Sure. Something Betty said about this cause map technique intrigues me," Henry commented. "She said that a cause map can serve as a group memory and makes it easy to pull others into your deliberations. I would like the Principal's Council to look at this and see if they have anything to add. Perhaps they will see something that we don't."

Figure III.10   Portion of Smartberg's Cause Map with Some Evidence

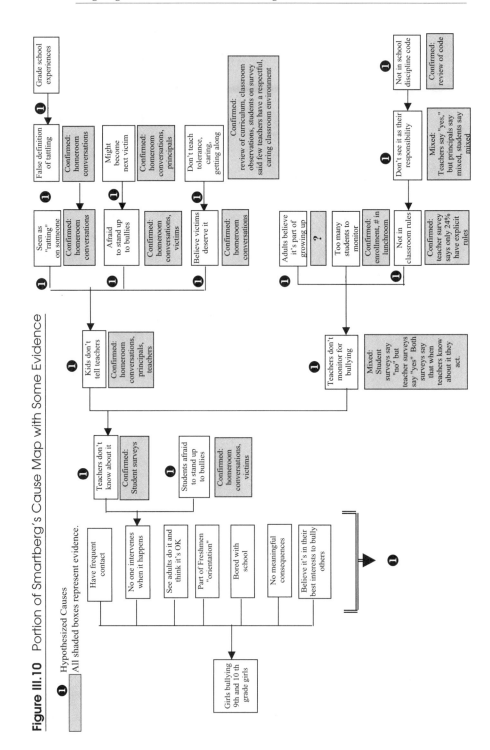

"Who else do you think should see this map?" asked Cheryl.
"Let's ask the Council," Henry suggested.

5th Meeting of the CIBO Task Force

"Again, I want to thank all of your for your hard work," Henry said as he opened the meeting. "Did you all get a copy of the cause map Cheryl sent out?"

Around the table, members pulled out their copies of the cause map. Some of them checked it against the map that still remained on the conference room wall.

"Today, we need to fill in our evidence question marks and then decide which confirmed causes we want to tackle first," Henry continued. "Oh, and I almost forgot, Cheryl also summarized our findings. Here's a copy of a chart she made for all of you," Henry passed out the sheet. (See Figure III.11.)

Figure III.11 Portion of Smartberg's Problem Is/Is Not Chart

The 'Queen Bee' Bullying IS caused by:	The Bullying is NOT caused by:
Having frequent contact (classes, lunch, lockers)	
Teachers not knowing about the bullying so they can stop it.	
Students not telling teachers about the bullying because they see it as ratting on someone.	
Student holding a false definition of tattling.	
Students not telling because they are afraid to stand up to the bullies.	
Some students not telling because they believe the victims deserve it.	

"You'll notice that we don't yet have anything listed on the NOT side of this summary. So far we haven't refuted any of our causes. Perhaps when we hear the new evidence that you all gathered this past week, we can put something in that column."

"Well, the evidence I collected won't fall into the NOT column," said Kathie. "I asked some elementary teachers about how they deal with the issue of tattling and they were very emphatic. They told me that their colleagues do talk to students about when it's appropriate to tell an adult about something that's wrong. They also told me that the counselors spend time in each classroom helping children learn when they should tell something to an adult. The counselors particularly stress this during their sessions on good touches, bad touches, when they talk about sexual abuse."

Kathie paused and then continued. "But despite all this explicit teaching some teachers feel that the message isn't getting across to students. Elementary students are still very reluctant to tell a teacher about misbehaviors. The kids are afraid their friends won't like them if they do tell the teacher. So I would have to say that the evidence does confirm that the grade school experiences of our high school students does play a part in their unwillingness to tell us about the bullying."

"OK, so we need to add that to our cause map and to our Problem Is/Is Not sheet," Henry commented. Nicole, the recorder for the day's meeting, put a blue sticky note summarizing Kathie's evidence on the wall next to the cause labeled "Grade school experiences."

"What about our hypothesis that one of the reasons teachers don't monitor for bullying is that they believe bullying is just a part of growing up and they can't do anything about it? What did you find out?" Betty asked.

"I talked with principals and they said that from what they see and hear as they visit classrooms, walk the halls, and talk with teachers, that just isn't so," Henry said.

"That's what the teachers said as well," Scott added. "They don't see it as an inevitable part of being an adolescent. But most of them just don't know what they can do to stop it from happening. They act when they see it, but they just don't see all of it."

"The students I talked with say that the teachers don't like bullying and don't want it to happen," Lindsey reported. "It's just that the teachers don't know it's happening unless it is right out in the open, which doesn't happen too often. The bullies are really sneaky. They have ways of doing it so the teacher doesn't see."

"Sounds to me that our evidence refutes this possible cause," Henry summarized. "Now we have something we can put in our Problem Is NOT column and, Nicole, we need a pink evidence sticky note on our map."

The group finished filling in all the missing evidence and then worked its way across their cause map, moving from right to left, asking about each possible cause: "Does the evidence confirm, refute, or show mixed results?" They found that their evidence confirmed almost all their hypothesized causes.

Step 2: Determine the Causes.
      C: Which causes should we tackle first?

Continuation of the 5th Meeting of the CIBO Task Force

Indeed, evidence confirmed all seven of their causes located just to the right of their problem event: Girls bullying 9th and 10th grade girls. They knew they couldn't tackle all seven so they began prioritizing to decide which cause to first move to Step 3: Find Solutions.

"I have one other sheet to pass around," Henry said as he distributed a copy of Tool #5. (See Figure III.12 to view the completed form.) "We need to examine each of our prime causes in light of these three questions," Henry pointed to the questions written on the easel pad.

1. If we could remove a particular cause from the situation, would we solve the problem?

2. Which confirmed causes fall within our sphere of influence?

3. Does a particular cause have effects that go beyond the current difficulty?

Figure III.12   Completed Smartberg Tool #5

A: Confirmed Cause	B: If removed, would solve the problem?	C: Within your sphere of influence?	D: Has negative effects beyond current difficulty?	E: Assigned Priority
9th and 10th graders have frequent contact.	√ Would push the bullying elsewhere	Not practical now	Actually would cause more problems to separate	LOW
Most often no one intervenes	√	√	√	**HIGH**
Students see adults do it and they think it's OK.		√	√	MID
10th graders see bullying as part of traditional freshman orientation.	Somewhat	Somewhat		LOW
Students are bored with school.	√	√	√	**HIGH**
No meaningful negative consequences.	√	√		MID
Bullies believe it's in their best interest to bully others.	√	√	√	**HIGH**

"Let's look at the first cause you see on the sheet: ninth and tenth graders have frequent contact. If we could reduce their daily contact, would that solve the problem," he asked.

"It might," Scott quickly replied. "But I don't think the bullying would stop. They would just do it somewhere else where they do have contact. Plus we found out that much of this is happening over the Internet in chat rooms and via email. It's virtual bullying. They don't even need to have face-to-face contact to do it."

"But it would stop it happening here at school and that's what we want," Marla added.

"I think we want it to go beyond just stopping it here at school," Rev. Harold replied. "I remember Nicole saying that the students told her an emotionally safe environment means no bullying at any time, anywhere, by anyone, period."

Nicole signaled that he had remembered correctly.

"I suggest that we put a check mark in that box, but we should keep in mind that separating the ninth graders and tenth graders won't stop it entirely," Cheryl stated. "At best, such a measure can only lessen the likelihood of it happening here at school. It still can go on away from school."

The group agreed and everyone checked the Column B box on their sheets.

"I think we should leave the next box empty," Yolanda suggested. "We could possibly turn this school upside down and keep the ninth and tenth graders apart, but I don't see it as a practical thing to do now. Maybe we can do something next year about the students' schedules and where the ninth and tenth graders have their lockers, but I don't see us tackling this now."

Again the group agreed and moved onto the next box in Column D.

"I believe we should leave this one blank too," said Cheryl. "Having the ninth and tenth graders together for classes and lunch doesn't seem to cause other problems. In fact, I think separating them would actually cause more problems. Do the rest of you agree?"

She heard a round of "yeses" from the group.

"Let's see," Henry began to summarize. "This means we gave this cause only one check mark and a qualified check mark at that. Let's move on to the next cause."

"I definitely think this is a three checkmark cause," Betty said.

"What's your reasoning for saying that?" Kathie asked.

"First, if someone intervenes, no matter who is doing the bullying, where or when they are doing it, the bullies will stop," Betty answered. "Particularly if students intervene and let the bullies know that it's simply not 'cool' to act that way."

"I agree," said Sandra, "but I'm not sure these queen bees will change their behaviors so easily. I don't see it as being in our …. Let me see what do we call it?" she paused and checked her yellow worksheet. "our sphere of influence. That's right. I don't think it falls within our sphere of influence."

"I don't mean to imply that it would be easy to get them to change their behaviors," Betty replied. "I do think it will be difficult. However, I also believe we can do it. We already have some evidence that shows that the eleventh and twelfth grade girls see this bully behavior as childish. We just need to convince the ninth and tenth graders of that."

"Dr. Logan, you said that you think this cause should get three check marks. How do you see this cause having effects beyond bullying," Nicole asked.

"This attitude of 'It's not my responsibility. I can't do anything about it,' has many negative effects here in this school, and even in the future" Betty explained. "For example, students, who say 'I can't,' don't even try, whether it's learning geometry, going out for the basketball team, or solving a bullying problem here at school. Students who don't try, who don't take risks, become adults who don't try, who don't take risks. This has grave ramifications."

"I think we all see what you mean," Henry interjected. "Do we all agree that this one gets three checks?"

Heads nodded "yes" and the group moved on to the remaining causes on the sheet.

"What about this one, 'Students bored with school'"? asked Scott. "If we made school less boring, even exciting, would that solve the problem?"

"I would say 'yes,'" Rev. Harold answered quickly. "You know, an idle mind is the devil's playhouse. As Cheryl said before, if students are engaged, truly engaged in their learning, they won't have time for this type of negative behavior."

"Although it would take some big changes around here, making school meaningful to our students does fall within our sphere of influence," Kathie, the science teacher, added. "We teachers do have a say in how we teach and we even have some influence in what we teach as long as we cover the state's mandated outcomes and our test scores go up."

"And we know our test scores need improvement," Henry added. "I see this boredom cause as being at the root of a lot of problems around here—low test scores, excessive absences, too many drop-outs, teenage pregnancy. The list can go on. Do you all give this cause a three-check-mark rating?"

The group continued discussing and after another 10 minutes had produced the grid you see in Figure III.12. They decide to move all three high-priority causes to Step 3: Find Solutions.

Step 3: Find solutions.
          A: What are some possible solutions?

"We've got 30 minutes left," Henry remarked as he looked at the wall clock. "Let's review what we've done and take a look at what we need to do next."

Nicole, the recorder for the meeting, quickly summarized the group's decisions.

"Looks like we're at Step 3: Find Solutions," Scott announced.

"Finally we can get to solutions!" said Sandra. "I've been waiting for this for weeks." Others at the table nodded in agreement.

"I hate to disappoint everyone, but I don't see how we can come up with a decent action plan in just 30 minutes," Ellie asserted. "I don't want to work this long and now just slap something together."

"You're right," Cheryl added. "That's why, I suggest that we spend our last 30 minutes getting organized for what we need to do during next week. We all need to investigate possible solutions and then come back later to actually create our overall action plan," she suggested. "Remember our job is to recommend a plan to the Principal's Council. We can't just start implementing anything until we get their approval."

Sandra looked deflated. "You mean that we can still be weeks or maybe even months from actually doing something?"

"I know it feels like we're only creeping along on this. It really tests our patience, particularly when we know that students might be suffering," Cheryl said. "However, we aren't just standing around doing nothing. We're taking actions now to help the victims that we know about and more students are coming forward just because they know we've got this task force working on the problem. You even said that things are going much better for your daughter."

"Yes, and I thank you all for what you've done," Sandra said.

Cheryl continued. "But we all know that these actions are only stop-gap measures. They really won't put a stop to all this vicious bullying. That's why we formed this task force—to find solutions that will prevent bullying over the long haul."

"So what do we need to do to prepare for our next meeting?" Rev. Williams asked.

"First, we need to look at all the causes that lead up to our top-priority causes and make a quick list of what changes we need to make, not how we will make these changes, just what in general we need to change," Henry explained as he drew large circles on the cause map around the three priority cause clusters.

"For each of these contributing causes, we need to ask: 'What, in general, would we have to change to remedy this cause?'" Henry explained. "And Nicole, as we work, would you please write our suggested changes on these green sticky notes and add them to our cause map?"

Within 20 minutes the group had placed a green note beside each contributing cause. The process went quickly because in many cases they had to only slightly restate the cause into a solution. For example, the cause "Students believe that victims deserve what they get" became the change statement "Convince students that victims don't deserve bullying." (See Figure III.13.)

"We can't come up with viable solutions for all those in just one week," Marla stated incredulously as she surveyed the wall.

"You're right," Henry said. "I suggest that we spend the next month looking for possible solutions. This problem *does* deserve a well-considered action plan. November 11 we have a full day for professional development. I know that we can get permission for us to use that day as a work session. But that means that we need to spend the next four weeks talking to people, researching, and gathering ideas about possible solutions. Do you think we can come back together in a month and have enough information to draw up a good action plan?"

Figure III.13 Portion of Smartberg's Cause Map with Changes Needed Added

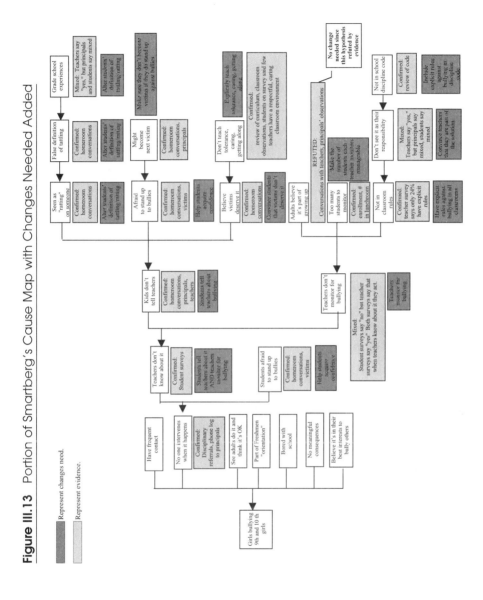

"I think that's possible," Betty answered. "However, I think we should split the tasks up among ourselves, form some small work teams around each of these priority causes."

"Good idea," Kathie nodded. "And I believe it's time we bring in some others to help us. We've been talking with lots of people and asking for their perceptions. Now it's time to get some of them to roll up their sleeves and join us in finding solutions."

The group spent the last part of the meeting organizing into work groups. Betty volunteered to head the team that would deal with the "No one intervenes" cluster of causes, while Yolanda's team would tackle the "Bullies think it's in their best interest" cluster and Kathie and Scott's team the "Bored with school" cluster.

The committee decided that each group would invite others to join the team, particularly adding those people who might contribute new perspectives or have a particular expertise. The group also agreed that all work teams would first look within Smartberg High School for possible solutions. Betty particularly wanted to talk with Pam Langer, the computer teacher, to see what she is doing to successfully prevent bullying in her classes even though several full "sting triangles" attend the same classes with her every day.

After looking within their school for solutions, the work teams would then check out what other area schools were doing. They would also search the Internet for possible solutions offered by experts, researchers, and other schools across the country.

Finally, the group outlined the contents for the work team reports. Each report would include a description of where the group searched for solutions, a recommended action plan (Tool #6), complete with rationale, and a tentative timeline for implementation.

"One final caution before we adjourn," Henry said as people gathered up their belongings. "As you search for solutions, try not to get emotionally attached to any one solution. Emotional attachments can cloud our judgments and close our minds to other possibilities. OK, thanks again and see you in a month."

During the month prior to the Inservice Day work session

The three work teams invited additional students and adults to join them in their search for solutions. Some members looked within the school for interventions that they might modify. Other members talked with staff at area schools, while others used the various search engines on the Internet to find possible solutions. They found the hotlinks at http://www.pittstate.edu/edsc/ssls/letendre.html especially helpful in sorting through the vast array of information on school violence and bullying.

> **Step 3: Find solutions.**
>   **B: Which solutions should we implement?**

The work team headed by psychologist Betty Logan faced a seemingly daunting task. Their charge required them to seek possible solutions to a page-long list of changes, all intended to remedy the "No one intervenes" cluster of causes. As they worked, however, they discovered that some changes actually would solve several causes at a time. For example, the change "Make sure students who stand up against bullies don't become victims themselves" would address three different but related causes:

- Students don't tell teachers about bullying when they see it.
- Students don't stand up to bullies.
- Bullies think they can get away with bullying others.

This discovery that one change can remedy multiple causes buoyed them up, making their task feel less daunting.

One week prior to the Inservice Day, all work teams held their own two-hour work sessions. They spent a portion of their meetings discussing the merits and feasibility of their possible solutions. They relied on the following questions to guide their deliberations:

1. Which solutions will give you the "biggest bang for your buck," solving several causes at one time?
2. Which solutions can you implement with current resources?

3. Which solutions represent remedies already in place that would just require a bit of tweaking?

4. Which solutions have shown to be effective in school settings similar to yours?

5. Which solutions meet the requirements of the change equation?

Each work team then took what they saw as their best solutions and drafted an action plan and a tentative timeline for implementation. The members tried hard to stay objective and not get too invested in any one intervention or program. They knew that, at the upcoming day-long work session, they might need to compromise and modify their recommendations.

6ᵗʰ *Meeting of the CIBO Task Force, 6-hour work session*

"Welcome everyone. We have a lot to do today. At the end of the day we want to leave here with a coherent, unified plan of action to address bullying here at SHS," Cheryl announced as she opened the meeting. "Let's introduce ourselves since we have the new members with us today."

After the introductions, Henry, who co-facilitated the meeting with Cheryl, reviewed the agenda. (See Figure III.14.)

"As you can see, the work team that tackled the cause cluster for 'No one intervenes' will present first," Henry explained. "Then we've allotted some time for questions. However, I would like to lay a ground rule about the questions. During this time, you should ask questions only to clarify your understanding of the proposal. I would like for us to stay away from judging the strengths and weaknesses of each group's recommendations until we hear from all three groups. We'll have the rest of the day to have those discussions while we work to mesh these three plans together."

Each work team then presented its plan. Each passed out a packet that included the group's rationale for its proposed plan, a draft action plan, and a Gantt chart showing a tentative timeline for implementation. As the groups presented their reports, members jotted down ideas on how they could integrate the various plans.

Figure III.14 CIBO Task Force 6th Meeting Agenda

Facilitators: Cheryl & Henry
Recorder: Sandra
Timekeeper: Rev. Williams

Starting time: 8:00 a.m.
Break: 9:45 – 10:00 a.m.
Lunch: 12:00 – 12:45 p.m. (Provided)
End of work session: 3:30 p.m.

What	*Who*	*How*	*Time*
1. **Review of minutes from last meeting**	Nicole	Oral report	5 minutes
2. **Review of the day's work session**	Cheryl	Oral report	5 minutes
3. **Report from "No one intervenes" solution group**	Betty	Oral report	20 minutes
4. **Questioning for clarification**	Everyone	Discussion	10 minutes
5. **Report from "Think it's in their best interest" solution group**	Yolanda	Oral report	20 minutes
6. **Questioning for clarification**	Everyone	Discussion	10 minutes
7. **Report from "Bored with school" solution group**	Kathie and Scott	Oral report	20 minutes
8. **Questioning for clarification**	Everyone	Discussion	10 minutes
9:45 a.m. BREAK			
9. **Decide on overall action plan**	Everyone	Discussion	2 hours
12:00 p.m. LUNCH			
10. **Breakout groups polish pieces of the overall plan and draft an evaluation plan**	Everyone	Breakout groups	1 hour 45 minutes
11. **Integrating pieces into overall plan**	Everyone		45 minutes
12. **Next steps**	Everyone	Discussion	15 minutes
3:30 p.m. END			

After the morning break, the group began drafting the overall plan. In some cases, people merged two solutions together to make a new, improved version. In other instances, they placed a particular solution on the back burner, on other occasions, the task force members forged an entirely new solution.

Throughout the work, Henry reminded the group that the overall plan must maintain unity of purpose, with all pieces of the plan working in unison. Members made sure that they did not propose something that might work at cross-purposes to another part of the plan.

By 11:30, the task force had drafted the beginnings of an overall plan. After lunch, the group fleshed out their plan and also created a tentative implementation timeline using a Gantt chart. (See Figures III.15 and III.16.)

Figure III.15 Portion of Smartberg's Action Plan

Date: _Nov 5_   Committee: _CIBO Task Force_

Confirmed Cause:
- Students don't have the confidence to stand up to bullies.
- Students belive victims deserve bullying.
- Students won't tell teachers.
- Students think it's OK to bully others.

Evidence confirming cause:
     Task force surveys completed by students and teachers, homeroom conversations, principal interviews

What do we need to do?	When?	Who will do it?	How will we evaluate the effectiveness of our efforts?
SHS team receives CASS training from Ophelia Project (Creating a Safe Social Climate).	December 1	Ophelia Project staff	Compare bullying incidents: last school year, this school year, next school year.
SHS team trains junior and senior girls in CASS.	December 8	Cheryl Nolan, Betty Logan, Nicole	Compare Healthy Kids survey results: last school year, this school year, next school year.
Upperclass girls conduct CASS sessions in all 9th grade health classes and 10th grade P.E. classes during 1st month of second semester.	Jan 15 thru Feb 15	Upperclass girls	Readminister CIBO Task Force surveys to students and teachers and compare beginning of school results to May results.
Expand Ms. Langer's "Random Acts of Kindness" Project schoolwide.	Dec. 1 to winter recess	Ms. Langer, Rev. Williams, Ms. Ryan, Ms. Sanchez, Mr. Chen	

Figure III.16 Portion of Smartberg's Gantt Timeline Chart

Place days/weeks/months along here ➔ TASKS	11-Nov	18-Nov	25-Nov	2-Dec	9-Dec	16-Dec	6-Jan	13-Jan	20-Jan	27-Jan	3-Feb	17-Feb
1. Get feedback from departments/PTA/Student Council on plan.	▨											
2. Make revisions to plan.		▨										
3. Take plan to Principal's Council for approval.			▨									
IF APPROVED												
4. Secure funds for travel to Erie PA for CASS training.				▨								
5. SHS team attend CASS training.						▨						
6. Select SHS upperclass girls for training.					▨							
7. Train SHS upper class girls in CASS.							▨					
8. Hold sessions in 9th grade health classes.									▨	▨	▨	▨
9. Hold session in 10th grade P.E. classes.									▨	▨	▨	▨
10. Create report Healthy Kids Survey results.						▨						

"I have an uneasy feeling about all of this," Kathie Warner, science teacher, commented. "I think we're trying to do too much too fast. If we look at each intervention separately, it's look very doable. But when I look at them all together—everything that we're asking teachers to do—I think it's overwhelming. Unless we back off on some of this, people will resist."

The group spent the next 30 minutes revising their overall action plan, making sure that no one group within the school would feel overwhelmed. They pared down some of their proposed interventions and delayed some until next school year.

"So where do we go from here? Are we finally ready to implement our plan?" Scott, the band director, asked.

"We're almost there," Henry replied. "However, remember the Principal's Council asked us for recommendations. The Council still needs to approve everything before we can put these things into place."

"Before we even go to the Council, I feel we need to share it with some teachers, students, and parents and see what they think about all this," Cheryl proposed. "We need their feedback to see if they are with us on our plan. As we said in one of our earlier meetings, we don't want to do all this work, come up with a brilliant plan, and then have it go down in flames because people won't back it. Any ideas on how we can get some feedback and yet have our recommendations to the council before the Thanksgiving break?"

The group mapped out a plan for getting feedback. The teachers, including the new members to the work teams, volunteered to share the plan with all departments during the next week. Sandra agreed to review the plan with the PTA executive committee on Monday night. Lindsey offered to take the recommendations to the Student Council and Nicole and the four other students, newly added to the work teams, volunteered to visit a handful of homerooms on Monday, Tuesday, and Wednesday.

The group set its next meeting at its usual time on next Thursday and drew up an agenda with just one item: Plow in people's suggestions and finalize the plan. They decided that Henry, Cheryl, Sandra, Nicole, and Lindsey would present the plan to the Principal's Council.

During Monday, Tuesday, and Wednesday of the next week, the task force members talked formally and informally with a wide variety of people within the school community. The plan received wide support and only a few people made suggestions for slight revisions. A week later, just prior to the Thanksgiving break, the Principal's Council approved the CIBO Task Force's plan to stop bullying at Smartberg High.

> ## Step 3: Find Solutions.
> ### C. Did our solutions work?

After giving approval, the Principal's Council assumed responsibility for implementing the anti-bullying recommendations. Before temporarily disbanding, the Caring In: Bullying Out Task Force fulfilled one more task. The members drafted a plan for evaluating the effectiveness of the school's interventions. Figure III.17 shows a portion of this evaluation plan. The task force members decided to re-

Figure III.17   Portion of Smartberg's Evaluation Planning Matrix

A Evaluation Question	B Information needed?	C Using what method?	D Who will collect?	E By When?	F How analyze?
1. Did queen bee bullying incidents decline?	Number of incidents reported over last year, this year, next year	Disciplinary referrals (last year, this year, next year), Behavior logs kept by teachers and counselors	Mr. Chen Ms. Nolan. Ms. Warner	On-going with reports at end of June, this year, next year	Line graphs, examine trend Line graphs, examine trend
	Prevalence, according to students, of queen bee bullying	Healthy Kids survey results Questions A63, A66, A68, A76-81 (last year, this year), CIBO first of year and end of year student surveys	Ms. Warner Nicole, Lindsey, Stu Co reps	March May	Test to see if significant difference between % last year and this year
2. Did more students feel comfortable reporting queen bee bullying incidents?	Number of incidents reported over last year, this year, next year	CIBO first of year and end of year student surveys	Nicole, Lindsey, Stu Co reps	May	Test to see if significant difference between % last year and this year

convene two more times during the remaining school year, once in the first week of March and again right after school was out.

March Meeting of the CIBO Task Force

Members of the task force greeted each other as they came into the conference room. Most took their usual seats around the table. Around the room pairs and trios chatted, catching up on the news since the last time they met back in early December.

"Look, they took down our cause map," Nicole said as she gestured toward the blank wall. "I wonder where it's at. Seems strange not to see it there."

"I rolled it up and stored it in my office just in case we need it later," Cheryl said. "Plus it's on my computer now."

"Let's get started," the group quieted down as Henry spoke. "Thanks for coming and welcome to our guests. Today we're going to take a look at how we're doing on our anti-bullying plan. Also Cheryl has a graph she wants to show us."

The group quickly plunged into their task. Principal Lyons, Pam Langer, Henry, and Cheryl reported that all pieces of the plan scheduled for implementation during spring semester were in place and going well after some initial fine tuning.

The group also examined a graph showing the number of reported bullying incidents from August to March 22 for last school year and this school year. (See Figure III.18.) The line for this school year showed two peaks: one in early September and one during early February right after the first anti-bully trainings took place with the ninth and tenth grade girls. The last two weeks in February, however, showed a quick drop off in the number of bullying incidents reported.

"This steep drop in bullying incidents might indicate that our training sessions with the girls are paying off," Cheryl speculated as she pointed to the graph on the overhead projector. "However, it also could mean that we're just experiencing a 'honeymoon' period. It's really too early for us to tell whether the trainings are making a difference. We need to continue gathering data and examine this again at our meeting at the end of the school year."

Figure III.18 Reported Incidents of Bullying as of March 22

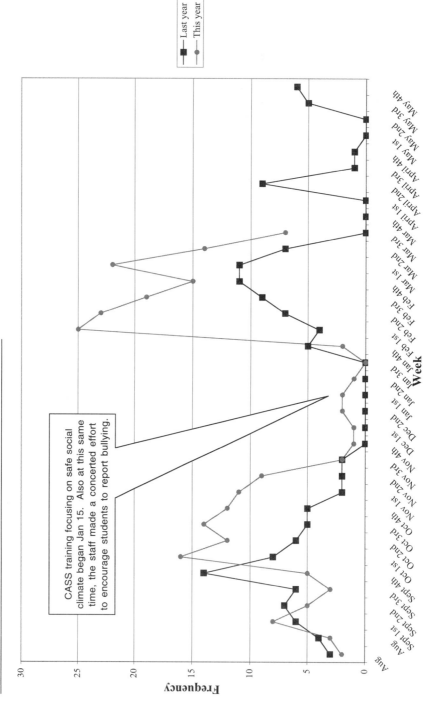

"I don't know, Cheryl, it just might not be a 'honeymoon' period," Ellie, the director from the "Y," interjected. "Look at this year's numbers compared to last year's numbers. Seems we might have a positive downward trend showing up this February."

"You might be right," Cheryl answered. "However, we'll just have to wait and see."

"I do want to say, Ms. Nolan, that I don't hear as many nasty comments as before," Lindsey reported. "I've even seen some ninth graders stand up to the bullies."

"Well, let's hope we've turned a corner on this," Sandra, the parent, added.

Throughout the spring semester, the students and staff at Smartberg High School continued their anti-bullying efforts. They also planned some major changes that would begin in August even before school started for the coming year. The Student Council spent many hours organizing a Week of Welcome (WOW) for the week before classes in the fall. They created activities, all designed to orient new students to the school and build camaraderie among both new and returning students.

In preparation for some of the WOW sessions, more girls received training through the Ophelia Project's® Creating a Safe Social Climate in Our Schools (CASS)[47] program. These new participants included some of the same "queen bees and wannabes" from earlier in the fall. To augment the CASS program, a cadre of teachers created a year-long series of activities that teachers would use during their homeroom periods to build trust and caring among students and adults alike.

The week after school dismissed for the summer, the CIBO Task Force reconvened for one more time. They came to the meeting armed with facts and figures gathered to answer the question: *Is our anti-bullying plan working?*

The committee reviewed an update of the graph they saw at their March meeting showing the weekly tally of reported bullying incidents. The data now extended out to the last day of school. In April, the students, parents, and teachers once again completed the short surveys the task force used during the fall to take stock of the bullying problem. Kathie distributed a summary of these spring survey results comparing them to the fall percentages. She also included the results of the latest administration of the Healthy Kids Survey.

All the data pointed to progress. Bullying incidents had indeed substantially diminished. The committee, however, realized that they needed to wait until next school year to see whether this trend continued and bullying really disappeared from Smartberg High School.

Part IV

Additional Resources

Chapter 1

Toolkit

The Toolkit provides blanks of various forms you can photocopy and use to make your problem solving easier. You can also download all the forms by visiting our website at http://www.pittstate.edu/edsc/ssls/letendre.html and alter them to suit your purposes. We have sequenced them, not in alphabetic order, but in the order in which you would need them as you use *Targeted Problem-Solving*.

Tool Kit

Table of Contents

Tool #1: Thinking Through Violence Worksheet

Step 1: Outline the Problem

A. In general, what's the problem?_____

Who (Perpetrators? Victims? By-standers? Any patterns?)	
What (Behaviors of perpetrators, victims, by-standers, adults. Any patterns?)	
Where (Physical location of the incidents. Patterns?)	
When (Timing of the incidents. Any patterns? Frequency)	

Impact on school's overall goals

Academic Achievement	
Physical safety	
Emotional safety	
Staff	
Parents/Community	
Accreditation	
Funding	
Facilities/Maintenance	

B. What outcomes are we striving for?

Student behavior outcomes?	
Teacher/staff behavior outcomes?	
Parent/Family, Community behavior outcomes?	

C. How close are we NOW?

> * Use Tool #2: Taking Stock Grid to summarize judgments.

D. Which gap do we want to solve first?

> • *Which gap, if we could solve it, would also close other gaps?*
> • *Which outcomes would require only a bit of concerted effort to get to a "5," fully achieved rating?*

Step 2: Determine the CAUSES

A. What do we think causes the problem?

> * Gather diverse perspectives asking *"What do you think causes the problem?"*
>   (Ask students, teachers, staff, administrators, parents, community members, and experts; review Taking Stock information from Step 1, Question C.)

> * List possible causes.

> * Zoom Out and Zoom In within the system to identify possible causes:
>   • *Is there any thing about our <u>curriculum</u> that's causing the problem? our <u>instructional strategies</u>? our <u>procedures</u>? our <u>policies</u>? <u>how we organize for learning</u>?*

>   • *Is something <u>schoolwide</u> causing the problem? within a <u>particular grade</u>? within a <u>particular classroom</u>?*

> * Build a Cause Map. (See Tool #3 for instructions.)

B. Which causes can we confirm with evidence?
   * Gather evidence through observing, asking, and reviewing documents.
   * Add evidence to Cause Map.
   * Summarize your findings using one of the techniques shown in Tool #4.

C. Which <u>confirmed</u> causes should we tackle first?
   * Complete Tool #5: Which Causes to Move to Step 3 Matrix
      * *If we could remove a particular cause from the situation, would it solve the problem?*
      * *Which confirmed causes fall within our sphere of influence?*
      * *Does a particular cause result in several key effects, all stemming from this same cause?*

Step 3: Find solutions.

A. What are some possible solutions?
   * List changes needed to remedy the causes.
   * Examine each cause and ask: *"How can we change or control this cause?"*
   * Search for solutions within and beyond the school.
      * *Is there something we are now doing that we can modify?*
      * *What have other schools done to solve similar violence problems?*
      * *What do researchers say?*
      * *Any ideas from the* http://www.pittstate.edu/edsc/ssls/letendre.html *website?*

B. Which solutions should we implement?
   * Determine which solutions to include in your action plan
      * *Which solutions will give us the broadest impact, solving several causes at one time?*
      * *Which solutions can we implement with current resources?*
      * *Which solutions represent remedies already in place and would require just a bit of tweaking?*
      * *Which solutions have proved effective in school settings similar to ours?*
      * *Which solutions meet the requirements of the change equation?*
   * Pilot test?
   * Complete Tool #6 Action Plan Form.
   * Complete Tool #7 Gantt Timeline Chart.

C. Did our solutions work?
   * Complete Tool #8 Evaluation Plan.
   * Use the evidence to judge the success or failure of the solutions.

      * If your evaluation shows success, congratulations!
      * If your evaluation shows the problem still persists, cycle back through Targeted Problem Solving, now asking the question: *"Why did our solutions not work?"*

Tool #2: Taking Stock Matrix

Directions: In Column A, list the outcomes you wish to attain. Then using evidence, judge where you NOW on each outcome. Place a • in the appropriate column. You may also want to add notes near your check mark to summarize your thinking. In Column B, list the sources of the evidence you used to support your judgments.

Column A: Safe School Vision Components	How close are we NOW to achieving our outcomes?						Column B: Supporting Evidence??
	No where near					Fully achieved	
	0	1	2	3	4	5	

Tool #3: Cause Mapping

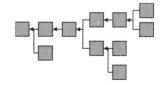

What is Cause Mapping?

In cause mapping you build a map that shows the cause-and-effect relationships that explain the violence issue you face in your school. The resulting cause map provides you with a visual summary of your thinking as you work your way through Step 2: Determine the Causes within *Targeted Problem-Solving*. The cause map also shows the evidence and the possible solutions associated with each confirmed cause of your problem.

What are some techniques for building cause maps?

Write it on paper with a pen or pencil.

> This approach works well if one or two people are working together to construct a simple cause map. For larger groups, you can use large sheets of paper such flipcharts or butcher paper on a wall to record your thinking. However, once you write down a cause, you can't easily move it to another position if you alter your thinking.

Use poly static cling sheets.

> Recently we worked with a group that used large poly plastic sheets that cling to the wall (or any other dry surface) through static electricity. You need no tape or push pins. We found that these sheets overcame some of the disadvantages of regular chart paper. First, if you use dry erase markers, you can erase your work and make changes. Second, you can easily rearrange these charts as you work. Finally, these cling sheets take up less room than paper when you fold or roll them for storage. The cling sheets come in perforated pads of 35 sheets that measure 27 inches by 34 inches and you can buy them at your local or online office supply store.

Use sticky notes.

> Writing possible causes on sticky notes makes it very easy to move the causes around. You can use small sticky notes on an 8½ x 11 sheet of paper or on a desk if you have only three or four people building a cause map. For larger groups, we suggest that you use 3 inch x 3 inch or larger sticky notes, placing them on flipcharts or on butcher paper taped to a wall. This way everyone in your problem-solving group can see the cause map. Using a dry-erase board as a platform also works well because the sticky notes easily adhere to the board and stay up. The difficulty with using a dry-erase board, however, comes at the end of the analysis when you need a copy of the cause map to take with you. To remedy this disadvantage, we suggest putting paper or a poly cling sheet on top of the dry-erase board first and then post your sticky notes. Later, you can roll the sheet up and take it with you.

Make an electronic cause map.

> After developing some proficiency with creating cause maps on paper using sticky notes, your group might consider adding a PC and an LCD projector to aid in your cause-mapping process. On our website at http://www.pittstate.edu/edsc/ssls/letendre.html, we provide a tutorial on how to create a cause map in Microsoft® Excel using the Draw function. Having both a large piece of paper with sticky notes that everyone can see on one wall and projecting the cause map on another wall in the same room using Excel can help a group work more efficiently. As the group constructs the cause map using paper and sticky notes, anyone can walk up to the map and add causes. At the same time, one of the participants, not the facilitator, creates an electronic record of the cause map using Excel. This dual approach prevents any stifling of input. Furthermore, later you can easily distribute the digital map by printing it out or emailing it to people.

What do we need to do in preparation?

Obviously, before you can begin to build a cause map you should have completed Step 1: Outline the problem. The work you did in Step 1, defining the who, what, where, when, and impact on your school's goals, will serve as a foundation for your cause mapping process. Also, as you ask, "What evidence do we have to confirm this cause?" you will find that your taking stock data from Step 1 will often provide the evidence you need.

Beyond this prior thinking, you do need to consider some logistics that will make your cause mapping go smoothly, particularly if you will work with a group of five or more people. First, consider the room where your group will work. At minimum, you need a room with a large wall (approximately 6 x 8 feet) where you can hang some butcher paper sheets. The room arrangement should allow for everyone in the group to easily see this wall. Second, you will need to get the following supplies:

- At least two large sheets of butcher paper. (We suggest that you tape them together to form a large rectangle.)

- Sticky notes, 3 inch x 3 inch or bigger, in a variety of colors. (We like to color code items as we build a cause map and suggest that you have pads of white, blue, yellow, pink, and green on hand.)

- Marking pens. (You may want them in different colors should you decide to do additional color coding.)

- Push pins.

- Masking tape.

Finally, if you decide to create and project a digital cause map, you will need a computer loaded with Excel, along with a LCD projector and the necessary connecting cables.

How do we get started?

We have found the following steps helpful in building a cause map.

1. Using a distinctive color pen, say purple, write the problem event (such as "Too Much Fighting") on a white sticky note and place it about half way down near the left edge of your paper. (See ❶ in Figure IV.1.) We find it helpful to use colored ink to make this cause stand out since it represents the event that prompted our work.

Figure IV.1   Steps in Constructing a Cause Map

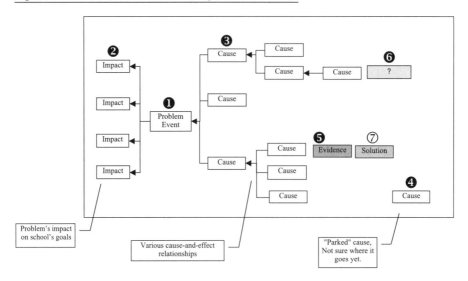

2. Next, go back to your work in Step 1 and lay in the impact this problem event has on your school's goals. These effects should go to the left of the problem event. (See ❷ Figure IV.1.)

Now, where do we go?

Once you have placed on your cause map the sticky notes for your problem event and its impact, you begin to work backwards, brainstorming the possible causes of your violence problem. We suggest that you write each possible cause on a separate white sticky note. People will generally begin by citing what they see as the direct cause of the problem. They may even use language like, "That's not the cause. This is the cause." Refrain from making judgments; indeed, welcome different points of view. Later in the cause-mapping process, the group will use evidence to either confirm or refute each cause. So for now, simply record all causes and put the sticky notes in a vertical line just to the right of the problem event. Don't worry about the order. The group will arrange them in a few moments.

Either the group's designated recorder can label the sticky notes or you can distribute pads and let individual group members write causes and add them to the cause map. Some people tend to say little in a group but have good ideas. If everyone has a pad of sticky notes, then anyone can offer causes by simply writing them down and placing them on the map, without saying a word. Letting people write their own possible causes allows quiet members to give input, but later you may need to do some culling to remove duplicates. A word of caution: Make sure everyone, even those in the back, can read the sticky notes. Keep the writing large enough and use large sticky notes. The power of doing a cause map as a group relies on the ability of everyone to contribute and those who can't see the map will often simply drop out of the discussion.

Once the group has generated approximately 10 to 15 possible causes, pause and have the group arrange the causes into plausible cause-and-effect relationships. (See ❸ Figure IV.1.) Resume asking the group for possible causes and pausing periodically to arrange the generated causes. If the group can't decide where to place a possible cause, simply park it over on the right side and come back to it later. (See ❹ Figure IV.1) We prefer to follow this "take-a-bit-and-arrange" process because we have found that if people generate too many causes at once, the sheer number often overwhelms them and stymies the process.

Continue generating possible causes and arranging them, until no one has any more to add. As you work backwards toward the right side of your cause map, you may generate additional causes by asking:

    a. What causes this?

    b. Why did this happen?

    c. What is required for this to happen?

You also want to make sure to ask yourself the Zooming In and Zooming Out questions listed on the Thinking Through Violence Worksheet, Tool #1:

    a. Is there anything about our curriculum that's causing the problem? Our instructional strategies? Our procedures? Our policies? How we organize for learning?

    b. Is something school-wide causing the problem? Within a particular grade? Within a particular classroom? About a certain subgroup of students?

At this point, you're probably wondering, "When do we stop generating possible causes?" The goal in cause mapping is to add as much detail as necessary, not to add as much detail as possible. If you can solve the problem effectively with three causes, then you don't need to add more causes to your cause map. However, we want to warn you that school violence problems, because of their complexity, often demand an extensive cause map with many more than three causes.

Once you have your possible causes arranged, you now examine each, deciding whether the evidence confirms or refutes the cause. Summarize your evidence on a sticky note and place it next to its cause on the map. (See ❺ Figure V.1.) We suggest that you color code your evidence by using a blue sticky to summarize confirming evidence and a pink one to indicate evidence that refutes the cause. If you don't yet have any credible evidence or the evidence is mixed, put up a yellow sticky note with a question mark on it. (See ❻ Figure V.1.)

After you determine the confirmed causes of your violence problem, you need to decide which of these causes you wish to move to Step 3. In Step 3, you will brainstorm possible solutions and once again use the cause map to document your thinking. Using green sticky notes, you then state the general changes you need to make and also add possible solutions beside your confirmed causes. (See ⑦ Figure V.1.)

How can we save our work?

You will find that as you work your way through the steps in *Targeted Problem-Solving*, you will rely on your cause map to keep you on track and remind you of your past work. We suggest that you leave your cause map posted on the meeting room wall so you can refer to it during later meetings. If you can't leave it displayed, then roll it up and put it up again before each meeting.

However, a word of caution: Over time sticky notes do come unstuck. To avoid a jumble of notes falling to the floor when you unroll your map, we suggest that before you roll it up, tape each sticky note in place with masking tape. The same advice applies should you decide to leave your map posted on the wall for several weeks.

We also suggest that you archive your cause map by transferring it into an electronic file in Excel. Not only will this save your work, but you also can easily track various iterations of your map. Plus you can easily distribute it to others through email or by printing out copies.

Where can I go for resources on cause mapping?

At our web site, http://www.pittstate.edu/edsc/ssls/letendre.html, we include a copy of the cause map template you see in this Tool #3, plus the full cause maps for the Challenge Team example we used in Part II and the Smartberg High School in Part III. You can download all of these templates for free. Also on our website, you will find a PowerPoint tutorial on how to use Excel to construct digital cause maps.

Tool #4: The Problem Is/Is Not Chart and Force-Field Analysis

The Problem Is/Is Not Chart

Once you generate hypotheses about the causes of the violence problem in your school or classroom, you need to scrutinize them using evidence. A Problem Is/Is Not chart summarizes your hypothesis testing into two categories: What *is* causing the problem and what *is not* causing the problem. Those causes confirmed through evidence go under the IS column, while the refuted causes go under the IS NOT column. Your strengths also go under the IS NOT column. Figure IV.2 illustrates how a committee of teachers summarized the results of their hypothesizing about the causes of their students not doing assigned homework. In Part III, the Smartberg CIBO Task Force used an Is/Is Not Chart to summarize their confirmed and refuted causes. (See Figure III.11.)

Figure IV.2   Illustration of an Is/Is Not Chart of the Homework Problem

IS the problem	IS NOT the problem
Students haven't yet sufficiently developed a sense that they must take responsibility for their actions	Parent say they want their children to do well in school
	Parents recognize the importance of doing homework.
Parents are not aware that their children have homework.	Teachers give incentives for completing homework.
Some teachers give homework that students see as meaningless, busy work.	Some teachers give homework that students see as interesting and challenging.
Most parents are not home in the evenings to supervise homework.	

Force-Field Analysis

This graphic organizer summarizes the forces that work for and against you in a problem situation. The line down the middle represents the problem you're addressing.

Arrows pushing from the left ⟶ indicate forces contributing to the problem. *Confirmed* causes go on this left side. Arrows pushing from the right ⟵ represent forces that work to eliminate or minimize the problem. Strengths working for you go on this right side. Figure IV.3 shows the force-field analysis a team of educators constructed to summarize their findings concerning the problem that students often fail to complete their homework. In Part II Chapter 2, Figure II.13 shows a force-field analysis chart some of Cory's students constructed to summarize their analysis of the teasing problem.

Figure IV.3   Illustration of a Force-field Analysis of the Homework Problem

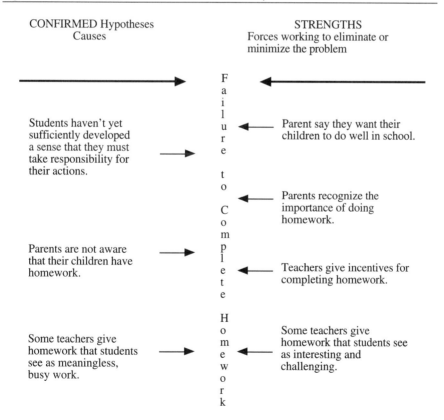

CONFIRMED Hypotheses Causes

STRENGTHS
Forces working to eliminate or minimize the problem

Failure to Complete Homework

Students haven't yet sufficiently developed a sense that they must take responsibility for their actions.

Parent say they want their children to do well in school.

Parents recognize the importance of doing homework.

Parents are not aware that their children have homework.

Teachers give incentives for completing homework.

Some teachers give homework that students see as meaningless, busy work.

Some teachers give homework that students see as interesting and challenging.

Tool #5: Which Causes to Move to Step 3 Matrix

Directions: For each confirmed cause, put a √ in each column where you can answer "Yes." After reviewing all causes, assign a priority rating to each.

√√√ = HIGH priority overall
√√ = MID priority
no √ or √ = LOW priority

Confirmed Causes	If removed, would solve the problem?	Within your sphere of influence?	Has negative effects beyond current difficulty?	Assigned Priority

Tool #6: Action Plan

Date: _____   Committee: _____

Confirmed Cause:

Evidence confirming cause:

What do we need to do?	When?	Who will do it?	How will we evaluate the effectiveness of our efforts?

Tool #7: Gantt Timeline Chart

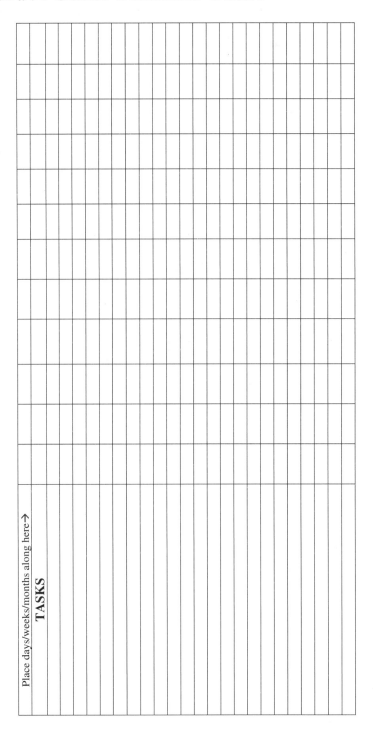

Tool #8: Evaluation Planning Matrix

A Evaluation Question	B Information needed?	C Using what method?	D Who will collect?	E By When?	F How analyze?

Chapter 2

Supporting Website

To augment this book, we maintain a website at <u>http://</u> <u>www.pittstate.edu/edsc/ssls/letendre.html</u>. Here you will find all the tools in the Toolkit ready for downloading. We also include an online tutorial that teaches you step-by-step how to create cause maps using Microsoft® Excel. At this website, you can also view the full cause maps for the Challenge Team example in Part II and the Smartberg High example we used in Part III.

Finally, we include annotations for valuable resources, both in print and on the Internet, that provide information about the following topics:

- statistics on the current state of violence in America's schools,
- school site safety audits,
- school climate surveys,
- crisis plan development, and
- bullying.

With a simple click of your mouse you go to the websites of publishers or visit recommended websites. We will regularly verify each of the sites we recommend and add others. This way we can keep our recommended resource list current.

Appendix A

"6 Steps to a Solution"

by Brenda G. LeTendre
from *Journal of Staff Development*
Winter 2000

at issue

D   A   T   A

6 STEPS
TO A SOLUTION

By BRENDA GUENTHER LeTENDRE

"That's simply not true!" Beverly, a 3rd grade teacher fumed as she looked at the newspaper editorial. The headline read: "Area Elementary Schools Shortchanging Students." She quickly scanned the article and found that the newspaper had based its claim on the latest state assessment scores for the community's three elementary schools.

In math and science, students at all three schools, including Beverly's, ranked below the state average. "We are, too, doing a good job! I know our kids are doing better than these state tests show," she muttered to herself, vowing to raise the issue at the next meeting of the school improvement committee.

"Look, this block scheduling we've been using for the past two years appears to be the answer to our problems," explained Murray, a middle school teacher, to his fellow teachers during a school improvement committee meeting. "But I'm getting lots of grumbling from our high school colleagues. They say we just jumped on the fad bandwagon and our kids are suffering. The high school teachers believe our kids simply won't be ready for the rigors of high school courses. How can we prove to them that block scheduling is working and our kids will indeed be ready?"

"I don't want to have to do that again," Joan complained to the principal's secretary as she walked out of the vice-principal's office, where she left four very angry 9th grade girls. "That's the second time today I've had to break up a shouting match between girls during passing period. Is it me or does it seem that this kind of thing is happening all the time? We need to do something to stop this!"

Beverly, Murray, and Joan need answers. In the first

Guide can help educators reach an answer

Brenda Guenther LeTendre is an assistant professor in special services and leadership studies at Pittsburg State University. She can be reached at 303 Hughes Hall, Pittsburg State University, Pittsburg, KS 66762, (316) 235-4504, fax (316) 235-4520, e-mail: bletendr@pittstate.edu.

D A T A

scenario, Beverly and her colleagues need to take stock of their school, answering the question: Where are we NOW? How "healthy" is our school? In the second scenario, Murray and his fellow educators need to determine the effectiveness of block scheduling. They need to ask and answer tough questions: Is it working and should we continue using it? In the third scenario, Joan needs to ask questions and get answers, but her questions have a different purpose: To find a solution to a problem.

Getting answers to these questions requires that educators know how to collect, analyze, and interpret data. In other words, they need to know how to conduct a credible program evaluation so that they decide how best to meet the learning needs of all youngsters. Conducting a credible program requires that educators follow six steps:

1. Pose questions.
2. Establish judgment criteria.
3. Make a plan.
4. Gather data.
5. Analyze data.
6. Interpret the results.

These six steps can serve as a suitable guide no matter how narrow or broad the scope of an evaluation. They work equally well for both individual teachers who want to take stock of their own classroom practices and teams of educators who want to determine the effectiveness of schoolwide interventions. Finally, the process can guide both formal and informal evaluations, as well as formative and summative evaluations.

If there's one thing we've learned in the last decade of school reform it is this: Good schools don't just happen. They happen because the adults in them decide to collaborate on systematically collecting and analyzing data, and then take action based on their findings. The six-step program evaluation process outlined here can serve as a beginning guide that we, as staff developers, can use to support teachers and principals as they seize the data and make decisions.

Answers require data: collecting, analyzing, interpreting.

STEP 1:
POSE QUESTIONS

In Step 1, educators pose the questions that will guide their evaluation. At the outset, their questions will most likely fall into three categories – questions that take stock, determine effectiveness, or seek solutions.

Some taking-stock questions that can get an evaluation off to a good start include:
● Where are we now?
● How "healthy" is our school?
● How do we stack up against the standards?

If teachers want to determine the effectiveness of a strategy, they can simply ask:
● Did it work?
● Did we achieve what we set out to accomplish?
● Did it make a difference?

Finally, if their purpose is to find a solution to a problem, they can begin by simply asking:
● What's going on here?
● What's causing the problem?

As they generate questions, educators should spread their net wide. They should seek input from decision makers who decide the fate of the program as well as people who are affected, either directly or indirectly, by the intervention. Finally, they should review the program's intentions.

STEP 2:
ESTABLISH JUDGMENT CRITERIA

Step 2 requires that educators determine up front the criteria and standards they will use to make their judgments. Why do this up front? A primary reason has to do with the difficulty we have in separating feelings from facts. Often

stakeholders already have in mind some sort of criteria and standards they will use to judge the worthiness of the program. However, these criteria are often implicit and rarely well-defined. Furthermore, if stakeholders actually do define their judgment criteria, they tend to do so at the end of an evaluation, when their emotions are so mixed with the facts that they can barely tell one from the other. Under such emotional situations, we tend to make snap judgments based on gut feelings rather than data. To avoid snap, emotion-laden judgments, program evaluators explicitly state the judgment criteria and standards before they gather any data.

For example, Murray and his middle school colleagues in the example above might use these criteria to evaluate the effectiveness of block scheduling:
● Students on the block schedule will master a higher percentage of items on the state criterion-referenced assessment in reading comprehension, math problem solving, science knowledge, and expository writing than similar students who aren't on a block schedule.
● Students on the block schedule will show more engagement during academic classes than similar students who aren't on a block schedule.
● Students on the block schedule will demonstrate greater perseverance when faced with a difficult learning task than students who aren't on a block schedule.

Another reason for defining judgment criteria up front is that frequently these yardsticks will dictate the kinds of data evaluators need. For example, if the criteria for judging the effectiveness of the Drop Everything and Read (DEAR) program is "Our students will read significantly more fiction books during the semester," the teachers know they will need to collect data that show the number of fiction books read by students the semester before implementation of the DEAR program, as well as the number of books they read during the semester of implementation.

Educators can glean ideas for the judgment criteria and standards by asking

			EXAMPLE: Evaluation planning matrix

What is the value of math journals?

A EVALUATION QUESTION	B INFORMATION NEEDED?	C USING WHAT METHOD?	D WHO WILL COLLECT?	E BY WHEN?	F HOW ANALYZE?
1. Do students learn math concepts better by using math journals?	Some demonstration of student under-standing comparing classes that used journals and classes that didn't.	● Weekly quizzes	Me	11/15	I will calculate mean scores 11/17.
		● Student-written explanation of concepts	Me	11/17	I will calculate mean scores on rubric by 11/22.
		● Student questionnaire	Me	11/22	Kids will tally. I will do %s by 11/25.
2. Do students improve their problem-solving thinking by using math journals?	Some demonstration of student problem solving comparing those who used journals and those who didn't.	● Scores on ITBS math problem-solving action	Me from counselor	4/15	I will calculate mean scores by 5/1.
		● Scores on math problem-solving section on state assessment	Me from counselor	12/1	I will pull mean scores by 12/15.
		● Student questionnaire	Me	11/22	Kids will tally. I will do %s by 11/25.

stakeholders; reviewing checklists, standards, and guidelines; consulting with experts; reviewing the purposes of the strategy; and examining research.

STEP 3:
MAKE A PLAN

Once they have their evaluation questions and judgment criteria in hand, the educators-turned-program-evaluators are ready to make a plan for getting their questions answered. Essentially, they sketch out who will collect what data, by when, and using what methods.

They also need to specify how to analyze the data they gather.

Building a matrix like the example above is the easiest way to develop an evaluation plan. In column A, the evaluator simply lists each of the evaluation questions posed in Step 1. Then, using common sense mixed with knowledge of good program evaluation techniques, the evaluator builds the rest of the matrix. Even modest, informal evaluations benefit from planning.

STEP 4:
COLLECT DATA

Program evaluators use three basic methods to gather information:
● Reviewing documents or artifacts;
● Asking people for facts or opinions; and
● Observing situations and behaviors.

No matter which data collection methods they use, evaluators should keep them simple and reliable. "Simple" means relying on existing data when possible and making data collection easy for both those who provide the data and those who collect the data. "Reliable" means using systematic and impartial methods to gather data.

STEP 5:
ANALYZE DATA

Step 5 consists of three tasks: organizing, describing, and analyzing the data. Organizing data involves putting the data into some sort of frequency table. One way to organize test scores is shown on the following page in the chart, "I feel

most in control when I am..." The accompanying chart, "I can make a difference in my life," displays a frequency table summarizing data from a survey.

When describing data, both pictures and numbers work well. Some common graphs used to summarize and display data include bar charts, line charts, pie charts, pictograms, scatter plots, and box and whisker plots. Evaluators can also describe a set of data by using numbers. The mean, median, mode, range, and standard deviation can indicate both the central tendency and the variability within a data set. Spreadsheet computer programs can generate elegant graphs, and also calculate various measures of descriptive statistics in a flash.

In analyzing data, program evaluators seek to answer a range of questions. Some answers to these questions rely solely on logic and critical thinking, while others also require analysis using inferential statistics. This is the point in an evaluation where technical knowledge

D A T A

about statistics and research comes in handy.

STEP 6:
INTERPRET THE RESULTS

In Step 6, the educators-turned-evaluators can finally answer the questions posed in Step 1. No matter what type of questions they posed, the evaluators should follow a similar process to interpret the results of their analyses.

First, look for patterns. Do most of the student opinions point to a positive learning environment within the school? When do most of the fights in the hall occur? Do students on the block schedule achieve as well as or better than those not on that schedule? Using some sort of summary matrix can often help evaluators see the patterns emerge.

Next, using these identified patterns, draw conclusions that will withstand the scrutiny of supporters and critics alike. Finally, apply the pre-established criteria and standards set in Step 2 and make judgments about the effectiveness and worthiness of the program.

As they interpret their findings, teachers and principals should be aware of various pitfalls that can render an evaluation useless. Some common missteps include:

● Seeing what they want to see, rather than the facts.

● Looking at the data only through a "microscope," thus failing to see the big picture.

● Performing only an "eyeball" test of significance and concluding that any change is significant.

CONCLUSION

The six-step evaluation process outlined above puts the power of data in the hands of those who most need it – the teachers and principals who are on the "front lines" with kids. The process prepares these educators for the implied seventh step in the process: Taking action to improve student learning, and continually re-evaluating the situation and the actions taken to see if modifications should be made. By helping teachers and principals acquire the skills of program evaluation, staff developers can cultivate educational professionals who use data, and not just instinct, to guide their classroom and school practices.

EXAMPLE: Frequency table

"I feel most in control when I am..."
ANSWERS TO A SURVEY OF 160 STUDENTS

A Possible choices	B Frequency *	C Percentage **
a. Sports	22	13.75
b. Alone in class	17	10.62
c. With group in class	43	26.88
d. At home	17	10.62
e. Other	26	16.25
f. No control	35	21.88

* Number of students who selected this.   ** % of students who selected this.

EXAMPLE: Frequency table

"I can make a difference in my life."
ANSWERS TO A SURVEY OF 6TH GRADERS

A Possible scores	B Frequency*	C Percentage**	D Cumulative frequency	E Cumulative percentage
0 (I CAN'T)	3	1.88	3	1.88
1	5	3.12	8	5.00
2	8	5.00	16	10.00
3	0	0.00	16	10.00
4	11	6.88	27	16.88
5	15	9.38	42	26.25
6	23	14.37	65	40.62
7	1	0.62	66	41.25
8	8	5.00	74	46.25
9	3	1.88	77	48.12
10	31	19.38	18	67.50
11	15	9.38	123	76.88
12	16	10.00	139	86.87
13	0	0.00	139	86.87
14	0	0.00	139	86.87
15	3	1.88	142	88.75
16	6	3.75	148	92.50
17	9	5.62	157	98.12
18	1	0.62	158	98.75
19	2	1.25	160	100.00
20 (I CAN)	0	0.00	160	100.00

*Number of students who obtained this score.
**% of students who obtained this score.

D   A   T   A

Resources for using data

Here is a list of recommended print and Internet resources on using data to guide instructional decisions. Many of these resources can serve as jumping-off points for educators who are just beginning to explore data-driven decision-making. You can access a more complete list of resources at author Brenda LeTendre's web site: www.pittstate.edu/edsc/ssls/letendre.html.

GUIDES

● **Fundamentals of descriptive statistics,** by Z.C. Holcomb. Los Angeles: Pyrczak Publishing, 1997.

● **Statistics: A spectator sport** (2nd ed.), by R.M. Jaeger. Thousand Oaks, CA: Sage, 1990.

● **Making sense of statistics: A conceptual overview,** by F. Pyrczak. Los Angeles: Pyrczak Publishing, 1995.

INTERNET RESOURCES

● **CLEARINGHOUSE ON ASSESSMENT AND EVALUATION**
http://ericae.net/intass.htm
Connects to the home page of the Clearinghouse on Assessment and Evaluation, sponsored by the Educational Resources Information Center (ERIC) funded by the U.S. Department of Education. A great jumping-off site to a myriad of topics all related to assessment and program evaluation. Simply click on the category of your choice and immediately you see links to quality Internet resources on the topic. A sampling of categories includes: action research, achievement data, alternative assessment, fairness in testing, goals and standards, instructional and program evaluation, organizations, pedagogy in educational measurement (much how-to stuff here), qualitative research, statistics, test descriptions, test reviews, and tests online.

● **GLASS, GENE**
http://olam.ed.asu.edu/~glass/502/
Connects to Professor Glass' web site supporting his course "Introduction to Quantitative Methods" taught at the College of Education at Arizona State University. Provides clear explanations with graphics illustrating concepts dealing with data analysis. Periodically asks questions to check your understanding and then gives you answers. Includes links to other statistics resources for "another treatment" of the topics. Not heavy on the statistical/mathematical symbols. Concentrates on explaining the concepts, but does show how to calculate various descriptive and inferential statistics using a computer program.

● **METTETAL, GWYNN**
http://www.iusb.edu/~gmetteta/
Takes you to Professor Mettetal's web page at Indiana University-South Bend, where you'll find links to action research web sites. Also includes a handy piece called "How to report statistics, a quick guide."

● **TEST REVIEW LOCATOR**
http://ericae.net/testcol.htm
Connects to the Test Review Locator, a searchable database giving descriptions and reviews for various testing instruments. Sponsored by the federal government's Educational Resources Information Center (ERIC). Also allows you to search the 10,000 tests included in the Educational Testing Service (ETS) Test Collection. The Test Collection encompasses virtually all fields within education and the social sciences. Also includes a helpful document giving tips on selecting tests appropriate to your purpose.

● **TROCHIM, WILLIAM M.K.**
http://trochim.human.cornell.edu/kb/ANALYSIS.HTM
Connects directly to the "data analysis" section of Professor Trochim's "The Knowledge Base, An Online Research Methods Textbook" at Cornell University. The best site I've found dealing with data analysis. Covers the concepts and procedures of organizing data, describing data, and using inferential statistics. Great graphics, clear explanations, enough detail yet doesn't overwhelm the reader. Very user friendly.

PRINT RESOURCES

● **Data analysis for comprehensive schoolwide improvement by Victoria Bernhardt. Larchmont NY: Eye on Education, 1998.**
A dy-no-mite book!! Very practical. Written in easily understood language with a collegial tone. Thoroughly walks through how two schools (one elementary and one high school) used data to make decisions. Excellent illustrations. Gives suggestions on gathering, displaying, and analyzing data from the following dimensions: (a) demographics, (b) perceptions, (c) student learning, and (d) school processes. Illustrates 10 levels of analysis from "snapshots" to the interaction of multiple measures over time.

● **Put to the test: An educator's and consumer's guide to standardized testing by Gerald Bracey. Bloomington, IN: Phi Delta Kappa, 1998.**
One of the best explanations of standardized tests I've seen. Gives an excellent overview of the purposes and uses of standardized tests and then clearly explains how test makers construct norm-referenced and criterion-referenced tests. Also covers performance tests. Provides a

jargon-free explanation of how to interpret tests, complete with sample printouts. Also provides a brief but clear discussion of basic descriptive statistics.

● **A hands-on guide to school program evaluation by E.A. Brainard. Bloomington, IN: Phi Delta Kappa, 1996.**

Packs into 70 pages a good overview of program evaluation. Quickly walks through a 10-step process for planning and conducting an evaluation. A good "starter" book for teachers and administrators alike.

● **How to conduct surveys (2nd Ed.) by A. Fink and J. Kosecoff. Thousand Oaks, CA: Sage, 1998.**

Very user friendly and makes the assumption that the reader is an intelligent person who happens to be naive about conducting surveys. Covers the process from start to finish, from planning to designing to conducting to analyzing to presenting findings. Includes many real world examples. Gives an excellent overview of how to do various statistical analyses of survey data. Can act as good reference on doing survey research and evaluation, since you can easily turn to the section you want and get the information you need.

● **Action research: An educational leader's guide to school improvement by J. Glanz. Norwood, MA: Christopher-Gordon, 1998.**

Grew out of the author's experience in teaching a graduate course on educational research. Deals with both research and program evaluation, with the purpose of creating reflective practitioners. Ably guides the educator through the research process, from identifying what to study, selecting a research design, collecting data and finally analyzing and interpreting data. Hits that happy medium between too much and too little information. Includes periodic exercises (with answers provided) so that you can check your understanding of concepts.

This article is based on material presented in two books:

● *Getting answers to your questions: An elementary educators' guide to program evaluation,* by Brenda G. LeTendre and Richard P. Lipka. Norwood, MA: Christopher-Gordon. In press.

● *Getting answers to your questions: A middle-level educators' guide to program evaluation,* by Brenda G. LeTendre and Richard P. Lipka. Norwood, MA: Christopher-Gordon, 1999.

For information, contact: Christopher-Gordon Publishers, 1502 Providence Highway, Suite 12, Norwood, MA 02062, (800) 934-8322.

● **Tracking your school's success: A guide to sensible evaluation by J.L. Herman and L. Winters.Thousand Oaks, CA: Corwin, 1992.**

Written for practitioners (both teachers and administrators) interested in whole school improvement. Focuses on providing educators with the guidance and tools to answers the following questions: How are we doing? How can we improve? How can we share our successes? Includes an annotated list of suggested readings at the end of each chapter.

● **Art of classroom inquiry by R.S. Hubbard and B.M. Power. Portsmouth, NH: Heinemann, 1993.**

Targets practicing teachers (Pre-K-12) who wish to conduct research that will inform their work with children. Written in a collegial tone with many detailed samples of data collection and data analysis techniques. Examples come from the work of practicing teacher-researchers (listed in the appendices of

the book). Chapter 2 covers note taking while "kid watching," surveys, student work and classroom artifacts, sociograms (one of the best explanations and examples of how to do this and what it tells you as a teacher), and the use of audio and video tape transcriptions. Chapter 3 includes a good discussion of how to find and refine a research question.

● **Making schools smarter: A system for monitoring school and district progress by K. Leithwood & R. Aitken. Thousand Oaks, CA: Corwin, 1995.**

Provides a comprehensive guide for taking stock of your school or district. Includes judgment criteria as well as suggested indicators dealing with the following areas: mission, goals, organizational culture, strategic planning, management, leadership, instructional services, decision making, policies, procedures, and school-community relations at both the district and school levels. Also provides sample surveys that you could use to collect the data you need to make your judgments.

● **Practical action research for change by R.A. Schmuck.Arlington Heights, IL: IRI Skylight, 1997.**

Chapter 6 focuses on "Responsive Action Research" where an educator gathers data to help solve a problem.

Gives a step-by-step explanation of the action research process, along with two case studies showing how two teachers used the process to solve the problems of unresponsive students and poor relationships among students of different racial groups.

● **How to evaluate your middle school: A practitioner's guide for an informal program evaluation by S.L. Schurr Columbus, OH: National Middle School Association, 1992.**

A must for middle-level educators wanting to know if their programs fit the needs of their students. Provides more than 25 survey and observation instruments based on the characteristics of exemplary middle schools. ■

End Notes

[1]2 dead, 6 wounded in Kentucky high school shooting. (1997, December 1). <u>CNN.com.</u> [On-line]. Available: http://www.cnn.com/US/9712/01/school.shooting.folo/.

[2]Heard, K., Everett, K., Bromley, S., & Uyttebrouck, O. (1998, March 25). "I never dreamed it would happen here' False fire alarm led pupils, staff into gunfire." *Arkansas Democrat-Gazette*, p. A1.

[3]Martinez, J. C. (1999, April 21). "Triage doctor horrified School library full of shooting victims." *Denver Post Denver*, p. A-11.

[4]Smith, M. (1999, December 7). "Boy 13, wounds 4 in school shooting." *Tulsa World*, p. A1.

[5]Gold, S., Ellingwood, K., & Reza, H. G. (2001, March 6). "2 killed, 13 hurt in school shooting." *The Los Angeles Times*, p. A1.

[6]Finn, P. (2002, April 27). "Expelled student kills 17, self, at school in Germany." *The Washington Post*, p. A1.

[7]A timeline of recent school shootings. (Retrieved December 8, 2002). <u>infoplease.com</u>. [On-line]. Available: http://www.infoplease.com/ipa/A0777958.html.

[8]Poll: More parents worried about school safety. (1999, April 22). CNN.com. [On-line]. Available: http://www.cnn.com/ALLPOLITICS/stories/1999/04/22/school.violence.poll/.

[9]Poll: More parents worried about school safety. (1999, April 22). CNN.com. [On-line]. Available : http://www.cnn.com/ALLPOLITICS/stories/1999/04/22/school.violence.poll/.

[10]When asked on the 34rd Annual Phi Delta Kappan Poll Sept 2002 "What do you think are the biggest problems with which the public schools of your community must deal?" 13% of the parents with children in public school answered fighting/violence/gangs. From Rose, L.C. & Gallup, A. M. (2002) The 34rd annual Phi Delta Kappa/Gallup Poll of the public's attitudes toward the public schools. *Kappan* [On-line]. Available: http://www.pdkintl.org/kappan/k0209pol.htm.

[11]Crosse, S., Cantor, D., Burr, M., Hagen, C.A., Hantman, I., Mason, M.J., Siler, A.J., von Glatz, A., & Wright, M. M. (2002). *Wide scope, questionable quality: Three reports from the study on school violence and prevention. Executive summary.* Washington, DC: U.S. Department of Education, Planning and Evaluation Service. [On-line]. Available: http://www.ed.gov/offices/OUS/PES/studies-school-violence/3-exec-sum.doc.

[12]Nationwide, 6.6% had missed at least one day from school during the 30 days preceding the survey because they felt unsafe at school or on their way to/from school. From Grunbaum, J. A., Kann, L., Kinchen, S. A., Williams, B., Ross, J. G., Lowry, R., & Kolbe, L. (2002). *Youth risk behavior surveillance—United States, 2001.* [On-line]. Available: http://www.cdc.gov/mmwr/preview/mmwrhtml/ss5104a1.htm. In a similar survey in Massachusetts, 8% of all students said they had skipped school at least once because they felt they would be unsafe at school or on their way to/from school. From Massachusetts Department of Education (2001). *2001 Massachusetts youth risk behavior survey results.* [On-line]. Available: http://www.doe.mass.edu/hsss/yrbs/01/results.pdf.

[13]U. S. Department of Education, National Center for Education Statistics. (1995) *The condition of education, 1995.* Washington, DC: U.S. Department of Education. Also see: Koplan, J. P.,

Autry, J. H. III, & Hyman, S. E. (2001). *Youth violence: A report of the Surgeon General.* [On-line]. Available: http://www.surgeongeneral.gov/library/youthviolence/chapter2/sec12.html#school.

[14]Wolf, R. (1999, May 4). "States act after school shootings. Some focus on prevention; others pass get-tough laws." *USA Today*, p. 3A.

[15]National Center for Educational Statistics. (1998). *Violence and discipline problems in U. S. public schools: 1996–97.* [On-line]. Available: http://www.nces.ed.gov/pubs98/violence/tab19.html.

[16]National Center for Educational Statistics. (2002). *Indicators of School Crime and Safety, 2002.* [On-line]. Available: http://nces.ed.gov/pubs2003/2003009b.pdf.

[17]National Center for Educational Statistics. (2002). *Indicators of School Crime and Safety, 2002.* [On-line]. Available: http://nces.ed.gov/pubs2003/2003009b.pdf.

[18]National Center for Educational Statistics. (1998). *Violence and discipline problems in U. S. public schools: 1996–97.* [On-line]. Available: http://www.nces.ed.gov/pubs98/violence/tab22.html.

[19]National Center for Educational Statistics. (1998). *Violence and discipline problems in U. S. public schools: 1996–97.* [On-line]. Available: http://www.nces.ed.gov/pubs98/violence/tab22.html.

[20]National Center for Educational Statistics. (1998). *Violence and discipline problems in U. S. public schools: 1996–97.* [On-line]. Available: http://www.nces.ed.gov/pubs98/violence/tab22.html.

[21]Koplan, J. P., Autry, J. H. III, & Hyman, S. E. (2001). *Youth violence: A report of the Surgeon General,* preface. [On-line]. Available: http://www.surgeongeneral.gov/library/youthviolence/chapter2/sec12.html#school.

[22]National Center for Educational Statistics. (2001). *Indicators of school crime and safety, 2001.* [On-line]. Available: http://www.nces.ed.gov/pubsearch/pubsinfo.asp?pubid=2002113.

[23]U.S. Department of Education Office of Educational Research and Improvement. (Fall 1999). *OERI Bulletin.* Washington, DC: Author. See also Cantor, D. & Wright, M. M. (2001). *School crime patterns: A national profile of U.S. public high schools using rates of crime reported to police.* Report on the Study of School Violence and Prevention. Washington, DC: U.S. Department of Education, Planning and Evaluation Service. [Online]. Available: http://www.ed.gov/offices/OUS/PES/studies-school-violence/school-crime-pattern.doc.

[24]Juvonen, J. (2001). *School violence: Prevalence, fears, and prevention.* Santa Monica, CA: RAND, 2.

[25]Crosse, S., Cantor, D., Burr, M., Hagen, C.A., Hantman, I.; Mason, M.J., Siler, A.J., von Glatz, A., & Wright, M. M. (2002). *Wide scope, questionable quality: Three reports from the Study on school violence and prevention. Executive summary.* Washington, DC: U.S. Department of Education, Planning and Evaluation Service. [On-line]. Available: http://www.ed.gov/offices/OUS/PES/studies-school-violence/3-exec-sum.doc.

[26]Crosse, S., Cantor, D., Burr, M., Hagen, C.A., Hantman, I.; Mason, M.J., Siler, A.J., von Glatz, A., & Wright, M. M. (2002). *Wide scope, questionable quality: Three reports from the Study on school violence and prevention. Executive summary.* Washington, DC: U.S. Department of Education, Planning and Evaluation Service. [On-line]. Available: http://www.ed.gov/offices/OUS/PES/studies-school-violence/3-exec-sum.doc.

[27]National Center for Educational Statistics. (2002). *Indicators of school crime and safety, 2002.* Washington, DC: U.S. Department of Education, U.S. Department of Justice. [On-line]. Available: http://nces.ed.gov/pubs2003/schoolcrime/excsum3.asp.

[28]National Center for Educational Statistics. (2002). *Indicators of school crime and safety, 2002.* Washington, DC: U.S. Department of Education, U.S. Department of Justice. [On-line]. Available: http://nces.ed.gov/pubs2003/schoolcrime/figs.asp.

[29]Moeller, T. G. (2001). *Youth aggression and violence: A psychological approach.* Mahwah, NJ: Lawrence Erlbaum.

[30]Sylwester, R. (1995). *A celebration of neurons.* Alexandria, VA: Association for Supervision and Curriculum Development.

[31]Alsaker, F. & Olweus, D. (2002). Stability and change in global self-esteem and self-related affect. In Brinthaupt, T. M. & Lipka, R. P. (Eds.), *Understanding early adolescent self and identity,* pp. 193–223). Albany, NY: State University of New York Press.

[32]Moeller, T. G. (2001). *Youth aggression and violence: A psychological approach.* Mahwah, NJ: Lawrence Erlbaum.

[33]Ibid.

[34]Loeber, R., and D. Hay. (1997). Key issues in the development of aggression and violence from childhood to early adulthood. *Annual Review of Psychology, 48,* 371–410.

[35]United States Secret Service and United States Department of Education. (Fall 2000). *Safe school initiative final report.* [Online]. Available: http://www.ed.gov/offices/OESE/SDFS/ preventingattacksreport.pdf.

[36]Moeller, T. G. (2001). *Youth aggression and violence: A psychological approach.* Mahwah, NJ: Lawrence Erlbaum.

[37]Astor, R. A., Meyer, H. A., & Pitner, R.O. (1999, April). *Elementary and middle school students' perceptions of safety: An examination of violence-prone school sub-contexts.* Paper presented at the American Educational Research Association annual conference, Montreal, Canada.

[38]Moeller, T. G. (2001). *Youth aggression and violence: A psychological approach.* Mahwah, NJ: Lawrence Erlbaum.

[39]United States Secret Service and United States Department of Education. (Fall 2000). *Safe school initiative final report.* [Online]. Available: http://www.ed.gov/offices/OESE/SDFS/ preventingattacksreport.pdf.

[40]Covey, S. R. (1992). *Principled-centered leadership.* New York: Simon & Schuster, Inc.

[41]Barnhart, C. L. (Ed.). (1963). The American College Dictionary. New York: Random House, Inc.

[42]Wiseman, R. (2002). *Queen bees and wannabes: Helping your daughter survive cliques, gossip, boyfriends, and other realities of adolescence.* New York: Crown Publishers.

[43]Ibid.

[44]"The Ophelia Project® is dedicated to creating a culture that is emotionally, physically, and socially safe, where girls are respected and nurtured. Through awareness, education, and advocacy, The Ophelia Project® promotes positive change in families, schools, and communities. By supporting a network of friends, mentors, and professionals, we encourage all children to become confident and healthy." Taken from the organization's website at http://www.opheliaproject.org/. The project's mailing address is: The Ophelia Project, P.O. Box 8736, Erie, PA 16505-0736.

[45]The number of students you need to survey to achieve an acceptable margin of error depends on the total enrollment of your school. Smartberg's enrollment sits at about 1000 students. According to statistical tables, the task force would need to survey 516 students (roughly half) to achieve a margin of error of ±3 percentages points at a 95% confidence level when generalizing the selected students' statements to the whole population of students.

[46]Healthy Kids Survey (HKS) "This modular survey can be used to conduct a comprehensive assessment of health-related risks and resilience among youth age 11 and older. It can be easily customized to meet local interests and needs. The topics covered include use of alcohol, tobacco, and other drugs; violence, weapons possession, harassment, and school safety; nutrition and physical activity; depression and suicide; sexual behavior; and external and internal assets. It is designed to help schools and communities improve prevention and health programs; demonstrate need for program funding; meet federal Title IV requirements; and promote positive youth development, well-being, and academic success. Full-service technical assistance is available to help plan, administer, process, and understand the survey. Results are provided in a comprehensive report emphasizing the significance of the data and a key-findings

summary with overhead transparencies. Developed in collaboration with the California Department of Education, the survey is already available to all school districts in the state; it is now also available outside of California." From WestEd's website at www.WestEd.org/hks. For information about the survey and fees, call 888.841.7536 or visit the above website.

[47]Creating a Safe Social Climate in Our Schools (CASS). The Ophelia Project® has developed a training program and curriculum designed to help school communities combat bullying and aggression, particularly among girls. Staff from the Project train both adults and girls to lead efforts to change the social climate of their schools. For information about this intervention, visit http://www.opheliaproject.org/national_programs/national_CASS.shtml or write them at: The Ophelia Project, P.O. Box 8736, Erie, PA 16505-0736.

About the Authors

Brenda Guenther LeTendre,
Associate Professor, Pittsburg State University

Brenda Guenther LeTendre began her career as an educator in 1971, teaching language arts at a large inner-city high school in Dallas. She has taught students at all grade levels from first to post-secondary and served as a central office administrator. In 1986, while pursuing her doctoral degree at Stanford University, she joined Henry M. Levin and his team to start the first Accelerated School in the nation. Since that time, she has helped launch and support Accelerated Schools across the nation, particularly those in her home state of Missouri. Brenda's expertise lies in guiding educators in the use of data to solve problems and make decisions. Currently, she teaches full time in the leadership-studies program at Pittsburg State University in southeast Kansas. Brenda lives in Joplin, Missouri, with her husband, Dana.

Richard P. Lipka,
Professor, Pittsburg State University

Richard Lipka is a Professor of Education at Pittsburg State University in Kansas. A graduate of the State University of New York College at Buffalo (B.S., M.S.) and the University of Illinois (Ph.D.), he taught sixth grade as a member of a four-person team in Amherst, New York. Dick is a recognized expert on the topic of self-concept and early adolescence and has published seven books and over a dozen articles on the subject. Over the past 24 months, he has researched the issue of school violence and translated his findings into a series of workshops entitled "Kids Killing Kids."

Index